Englisch

Rätsel & Übungen *für zwischendurch*

Englisch

Rätsel & Übungen

für zwischendurch

Jetzt neu mit Verbtabellen

Weltbild

Genehmigte Lizenzausgabe der Verlagsgruppe Weltbild GmbH,
Steinerne Furt, 86167 Augsburg

Umschlaggestaltung: Atelier Seidel, Teising
Umschlagmotiv: Atelier Seidel, Teising
(unter Verwendung von istockphotos)
Gesamtherstellung: Bagel Roto-Offset GmbH & Co. KG, Schleinitz
Printed in the EU
ISBN 978-3-8289-2241-9

2010 2009 2008
Die letzte Jahreszahl gibt die aktuelle Lizenzausgabe an.

Teil 1

Johannes Schumann

Englisch ganz leicht

Rätsel & Übungen *für zwischendurch*

Vorwort

Wie oft hat man nicht zwischendurch mal ein paar Minuten Zeit zum Lernen! Im Bus, am Strand, im Café ... Nutzen Sie diese Zeit zum Wiederholen und Entdecken von Neuem. Mit *Englisch ganz leicht Rätsel und Übungen für zwischendurch* können Sie Ihren Grundwortschatz festigen und erweitern – eben auf ganz leichte Art! Dieses Buch bietet Ihnen 100 abwechslungsreiche Rätsel und Übungen (im Folgenden „Tests“ genannt) zu verschiedenen Themenbereichen. Die Lösungen im Anhang geben Ihnen die nötige Sicherheit und Kontrolle.

Denken Sie daran, dass es nicht wichtig ist, möglichst viele Tests hintereinander zu lösen. Prägen Sie sich jeweils nur einen Test gut ein – aber möglichst regelmäßig und am besten täglich. Markieren Sie, was Ihnen wichtig ist und was Sie lernen möchten.
Beim Wortschatzerwerb spielt die Häufigkeit der Wiederholung die entscheidende Rolle, damit Neues ins Langzeitgedächtnis übergehen kann.

Dieses Testbuch ist geeignet für erwachsene Selbstlerner, aber auch für Schüler, die in abwechslungsreicher und spielerischer Form ihre Sprachkenntnisse auffrischen wollen.

Wir wünschen Ihnen viel Spaß!

DIESE ARTEN VON TESTS GIBT ES

Hinweis: Einige Testnummern sind unter mehreren Rubriken genannt.

TESTS ZU BESTIMMTEN THEMEN

TESTS ZU WORTSCHATZ UND GRAMMATIK

TEST 1

Setzen Sie ein.

aloud application at be ~~cross~~ different duty fond German haircut map only pick pieces possible result send special travel work

1. den Fluss überqueren > to cross the river
2. laut lesen > to read ________
3. ich hole dich ab > I'll ________ you up
4. schwer arbeiten > to _______ hard
5. gern haben / lieb haben > to be _______ of / to like
6. verschieden sein > to be __________
7. Besten Dank für Ihre Bewerbung. > We thank you for your _________.
8. sich die Haare schneiden lassen > to have a _____
9. nichts Besonderes > nothing ____________
10. mit dem Schiff fahren > to __________ by ship
11. Bitte zeigen Sie mir das auf der Karte. > Please show it to me on the ___.
12. im Hotel übernachten > to stay ___ the hotel
13. in Stücke schneiden > to cut into __________
14. ins Deutsche übersetzen > to translate into __________
15. so bald wie möglich > as soon as ______________
16. holen lassen / kommen lassen > to _______ for
17. erst gestern > _______ yesterday
18. es ist meine Pflicht zu > it's my _______ to
19. es wird schon werden / gehen > it will ___ all right
20. zur Folge haben > to __________ in

TEST 2

Was passt links und rechts zusammen?

1.	flower	sugar
2.	car	lid
3.	train	ticket
4.	coffee	vase
5.	pot	boot / trunk

a)	soup	ski lift
b)	fever	mustard
c)	stairs	banisters
d)	sausage	thermometer
e)	snow	spoon

I.	bicycle	stage
II.	theatre	clown
III.	pub	beer
IV.	circus	leather
V.	jacket	bell

A)	zoo	music
B)	computer	star
C)	sky	animals
D)	disco	suitcase
E)	luggage	printer

TEST 3

Finden Sie Wortpaare mit gegenteiliger Bedeutung.

blunt ~~boring~~ bottom dirty down dry early empty happy light never old opaque poor rough rude short stale wrong young

1. interesting - boring
2. tall - __________
3. rich - __________
4. sad - __________
5. new - __________
6. smooth - __________
7. sharp - __________
8. clean - __________
9. up - __________
10. top - __________
11. fresh - __________
12. late - __________
13. wet - __________
14. old - __________
15. full - __________
16. right - __________
17. transparent - __________
18. always - __________
19. heavy - __________
20. polite - __________

TEST 4

Setzen Sie ein.

beginning Can Follow Keep listening money next ~~piece~~ quite receipt recommended taste test town tree Turn understand upset windshield

1. Was für ein Glück! > What a piece of good luck!
2. Das ist eine gute Gelegenheit, Geld zu verdienen. > This is a good opportunity to make ________.
3. das ist wohl möglich / das mag sein > that's ________ possible
4. Ich höre zu. > I am ________________.
5. Ich verstehe nicht. > I do not ________________.
6. Rechts fahren! / halten! > _______ to the right!
7. Meine Windschutzscheibe ist kaputt. > My ___________ is broken.
8. Die Prüfung war hart. > The __________________ was tough.
9. Sie ist deswegen so aufgebracht / verärgert. > She is so ______ about this matter.
10. Wie lautet Ihre Anschrift hier in der Stadt? > What is your address in this _______?
11. Hiermit bestätige ich den Eingang Ihrer Lieferung. > I acknowledge ____________ of your delivery.
12. bitter schmecken > to ________ bitter
13. am Anfang > in the ________________
14. Wo ist der nächste Abschleppdienst? > Where is the ______ towing service?
15. Können Sie mich mit dieser Nummer verbinden? > _____ you connect me to this number?
16. Folgen Sie der Straßenbahnlinie. > __________ the tram lines.
17. Er hat sie für den Job empfohlen. > He ___________________ her for the job.
18. Stell das Radio ab! > _______ off the radio!
19. auf einen Baum klettern > to climb up a _______

TEST 5

Finden Sie die logische Entsprechung.

Arabic baker Bulgaria captain ~~church~~ continent death dwarf earth eat forbid French future listen milk mouth ocean restaurant river south

1. actor : theatre = priest : church
2. aeroplane : pilot = ship : ____________________
3. air : to breathe = food : to ____________________
4. Alps : mountain range = Nile : ____________________
5. yes : no = to allow : to ____________________
6. Ankara : Turkey = Sofia : ____________________
7. Arctic : north = Antarctic : ____________________
8. Astronomy : space = Geology : ____________________
9. Rhine : river = Atlantic : ____________________
10. Australia : English = Egypt : ____________________
11. Germany : German = France : ____________________
12. hair salon : hair dresser = bakery : ____________________
13. bee : honey = cow : ____________________
14. beginning : end = birth : ____________________
15. behind : front = past : ____________________
16. Belgium : country = Europe : ____________________
17. Bible : church = menu : ____________________
18. big : small = giant : ____________________
19. bird : beak = human : ____________________
20. book : to read = music : to ____________________

TEST 6

Finden Sie waagerecht oder senkrecht 11 Farben.

g	**r**	**e**	**e**	**n**	w	b	d	a
e	b	r	o	w	n	l	k	w
n	p	i	n	k	u	u	j	h
r	p	u	r	p	l	e	o	i
u	g	c	a	b	m	v	r	t
g	y	e	l	l	o	w	a	e
r	j	w	m	a	l	r	n	e
e	z	g	l	c	w	e	g	i
y	s	b	u	k	c	d	e	c

TEST 7

Setzen Sie ein.

anything by cracked educated else equals fault head headache mistake cinema play right ~~scenery~~ speaks Sunday times to touch yesterday

1. fantastische Landschaft > fantastic scenery
2. ich kann nicht anders als > I can't do ______ other than
3. sechs durch zwei ist drei > six divided by two ______ three
4. der Kopf tut mir weh > I've got a ______
5. geschieht ihm recht > serves him ______
6. letzten Sonntag > last ______
7. die Scheibe ist gesprungen > the pane is ______
8. niemand anders / niemand sonst / weiter niemand > nobody ______
9. ein gebildeter Mensch > an ______ man
10. eine Rolle spielen > to ______ a part / to act a part
11. einen Fehler machen > to make a ______
12. mit dem Zug / mit der Bahn > ____ rail
13. im Kino > at the ______
14. in Verbindung stehen mit > to be in ______ with
15. ins Schwarze treffen > to hit the nail on the ______
16. er kann mehrere Sprachen > he ______ several languages
17. drei mal drei ist neun > three ______ three is nine
18. erst gestern > only ______
19. es ist meine Schuld > it is my ______
20. es wird sicher regnen > it's sure ____ rain

TEST 8

Was passt links und rechts zusammen?

1.	wall	finger
2.	hand	tennis ball
3.	racket	bulb
4.	lamp	peel
5.	banana	brick
a.	suit	goal
b.	computer	sugar
c.	football	tie
d.	book	mouse
e.	coffee	page
I.	Berlin	cork
II.	weather	beer
III.	night	darkness
IV.	thirst	city
V.	bottle	snow
A.	tree	slice
B.	television	trunk
C.	bread	rules
D.	leg	programme
E.	grammar	foot

TEST 9

Welches Wort passt nicht in die Reihe?

1. blue brown ~~hard~~ yellow
2. sun star cloud moon
3. resentful jealous envious happy
4. apples beans broccoli peas
5. Albania Belgium Benelux Bulgaria
6. apple-juice beer service coffee
7. pineapple spinach apricots pears
8. eyebrows moustache beard throat
9. August weather October November
10. bathroom kitchen street bedroom
11. badminton tree billiards boxing
12. farmer fisherman hunter architect
13. bananas strawberries petrol blueberries
14. Berlin Zurich Hamburg Munich
15. hill picture vase bookshelf
16. visit scream sing laugh
17. lightning thunder handwriting storm
18. Chile Brazil Argentina Uruguay
19. brush cream fork comb
20. computer belt glove shirt

TEST 10

Setzen Sie ein.

accept ~~accident~~ as beer collect do dog electrician enquiry floor French if later laughing mountain tooth varies water what will

1. Haben Sie den Unfall gesehen? > Did you see the accident________?
2. Lachst du oder weinst du? > Are you ______________ or crying?
3. der höchste Berg der Welt > the highest __________ in the world
4. Schluss damit! > That will ___!
5. wenn ich mich nicht irre > ____ I'm not mistaken
6. Der Elektriker hat unseren Fernseher repariert. > The ____________________ repaired our television.
7. Bezahlen Sie jetzt oder später? > Would you like to pay now or _________?
8. sich einen Zahn ziehen lassen > to have a _________ pulled out
9. Die Temperatur ändert sich von Ort zu Ort. > The temperature _________ from place to place.
10. Sie müssen warten. > You _______ have to wait.
11. Nehmen Sie Kreditkarten an? > Do you _________ credit cards?
12. Im unteren Stock. > On the _________ below.
13. Um welche Zeit? / Um wieviel Uhr? > At _______ time?
14. Möchten Sie ein großes oder kleines Bier? > Do you want a large or small _______?
15. voll Wasser > filled with _________
16. soviel wie möglich > ____ much as possible
17. Er machte die russisch-französische Übersetzung. > He did the Russian to ___________ translation.
18. Briefmarken sammeln > to _____________ stamps
19. Für Ihre Anfrage bedanken wir uns. > We thank you for your _____________.
20. Hunde an der Leine führen! > Keep your _____ on the leash!

TEST 11

Was passt zusammen?
Bilden Sie Sprichwörter oder Redensarten.

1. A barking dog	**a)** come to an end.
2. A bird in the hand	**b)** even when he speaks the truth.
3. A friend in need	**c)** in love and war.
4. A liar is not believed	**d)** is a friend indeed.
5. A single stroke	**e)** is not gold.
6. Actions speak	**f)** is worth two in the bush.
7. All's fair	**g)** lead to Rome.
8. All roads	**h)** louder than words.
9. All that glitters	**i)** never bites.
10. All things must	**j)** won't fell an oak.

11. All's well	**a)** a tooth for a tooth.
12. An eye for an eye,	**b)** is his castle.
13. A man's home	**c)** little fish.
14. You've made your bed,	**d)** now lie in it.
15. Better late	**e)** tell no tales.
16. Big fish eat	**f)** than never.
17. Brevity is	**g)** that ends well.
18. Caution is	**h)** the mother of wisdom.
19. Cold hands,	**i)** the soul of wit.
20. Dead men	**j)** warm heart

TEST 12

Setzen Sie ein.

benefit dishes down enter late love obliged only post read receipt second smoke ~~spend~~ succeeded such thinking this wake wine

1. das Wochenende verbringen > to spend the weekend
2. ich bin Ihnen sehr verbunden > I am greatly ____________ to you
3. ich koste den Wein > I'll taste the _______
4. Wecken Sie mich bitte um ... > Please _______ me at ...
5. den Brief einwerfen > to __________ the letter
6. der / die / das Zweite > the __________
7. das Geschirr spülen > to do the _______
8. die Zeitung lesen > to _______ the paper
9. ein Gespräch beginnen > to _________ into conversation
10. ein solcher Mensch / solch ein Mensch > _______ a person
11. eine Zigarette rauchen > to _________ a cigarette
12. einen Vorteil haben von > to ____________ from
13. Wir haben Ihre Reklamation erhalten. > We confirm ____________ of your complaint.
14. im Laufe dieser Woche > in the course of _______ week
15. an die Arbeit gehen / sich ans Werk machen > to get _______ to work
16. Woran denkst du? > What are you ______________ about?
17. erst heute > _______ today
18. es ist mir gelungen > I have ________________
19. es wird spät > it's getting _______
20. aus Liebe heiraten > to marry for _______

TEST 13

Kreuzworträtsel

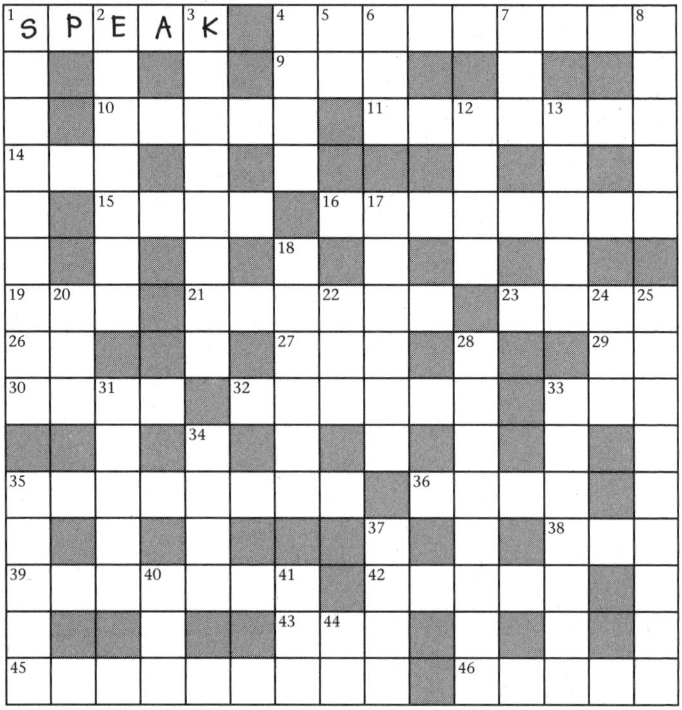

WAAGERECHT

1 Can you s**** fluent French?

4 The s******** carried many passengers down the Mississippi.

9 The child is crying because its t** is broken.

10 He has a mobile p****, but I don't know the number.

11 The doctor gave me some ear drops for my e******.

14 He can't s** without his spectacles.

15 We baked her a c*** for her birthday.

16 He's a s******* here, nobody knows him.

19 The child wants i** mother.

21 Wipe your hands on the n***** next to your plate.

23 That t*** has no leaves in the winter.

26 N*, he is not here.

27 E** is a popular seafood in this area.

29 I a* your new boss.

30 The orphanage g*** money from charitable people.

32 Hello! Is a***** home?

33 There a** many good pubs here.

35 I need some lemons and sugar to make l*******.

36 He bought a k*** of potatoes.

38 He's wearing a bow t** to the party.

39 She needs some driving l******, will you teach her?

42 Belfast is an I**** city.

43 I need some fresh a**, open the windows.

45 I need to smoke, I need a c********.

46 Go to sleep, you have to wake up e**** tomorrow.

SENKRECHT

1 Oregano is a good s******** in a salad.

2 He e****** to get the job without any difficulties.

3 I can hear someone k******* on the door.

4 She made a meat and vegetable s*** for supper.

5 Please give this t* him.

6 She uses a lot of e** shadow on her eyelids.

7 Her b** is visible through her white dress.

8 The children hugged t**** parents.

12 Have you r*** this book?

13 He hates cigarettes, but he smokes one c**** a day.

17 I had this suit made by a t***** in town.

18 She o***** the door and let them in.

20 He hurt his t** when his foot hit the door.

22 I can't find the k** to this lock.

24 He whispered in her e**.

25 This is an e********, please call the police!

28 Did the doctor prescribe any m******* for your pain?

31 How many t**** have you visited this museum?

33 This shirt is dirty, could I have a****** one?

34 They moved i*** their new house.

35 The colour l**** reminds me of lavender.

37 You t*** very easily, you have no stamina.

40 The sailor is away at s**.

41 She s** at the desk next to me when I was in school.

44 I* is very cold today.

TEST 14

Wilde Tiere

Welches Lösungswort ergibt sich in der senkrechten Reihe?

		R	H		N		C		R		S
		G		R		F	F				
			P		N	G			N		
	L		P	H		N	T				
		F		X							
L			P		R	D					
		W		L	F						
			T		G		R				
	B			R							
	C		M		L						
		T		R	T	L					
			S	N		K					

TEST 15

Setzen Sie die Buchstaben in die richtige Reihenfolge, um die logische Entsprechung zu finden.

1. bookstore : books = optician : [ssaselg] glasses
2. boxing : gloves = tennis : [takrce] ________
3. brave : afraid = bravery : [reaf] ________
4. Brazil : Brazilians = Mexico : [easixMcn] ________
5. Brussels : Belgium = Athens : [ereceG] ________
6. Buddha : Buddhism = Christ : [yiahtitsiCrn] ________
7. building : storeys = apartment : [omors] ________
8. bus : bus stop = train : train [tastoni] ________
9. campsite : hotel = cheap : [vexsnieep] ________
10. car : horn = bicycle : [lelb] ________
11. sleigh : horses = car : [neigen] ________
12. car : wheel = table : [elg] ________
13. lamp : ceiling = carpet : [oorlf] ________
14. cheap : expensive = canteen : [attuerrnas] ________
15. cheetah : fast = snail : [lwso] ________
16. chocolate : bar = truffles : [obx] ________
17. Christianity : Bible = Islam : [aornK] ________
18. church : to pray = school : to [dtsyu] ________
19. cigarettes : lungs = alcohol : [ierlv] ________
20. cigarettes : vegetables = sick : [elhthya] ________

TEST 16

Setzen Sie ein.

age been books change cut Catholic fastest finish Leave meat morning never only people placed running ~~so~~ stay used vegetables

1. ja, ich denke schon > yes, I think __so__
2. Haben Sie gekochtes Gemüse? > Have you got any cooked ____________?
3. man kann nie wissen > you ________ know
4. über Nacht bleiben / übernachten > to _______ overnight
5. Ich fahre morgen sehr früh ab. > I am leaving early tomorrow __________.
6. Ich möchte Braten mit Kartoffeln. > I would like some _______ with potatoes.
7. Geh aus dem Zimmer, damit ich Ruhe habe. > ________ the room so that I can have some peace.
8. sehr viele Leute > a great many __________
9. Der Rest ist für Sie. / Stimmt so. > Keep the __________.
10. sich in den Finger schneiden > to _____ one's finger
11. Dieser Athlet läuft am schnellsten. > This athlete runs the __________.
12. wir sind gleich alt > we are the same _____
13. Sind Sie Katholik oder Protestant? > Are you ______________ or Protestant?
14. mit fließendem Wasser > with ____________ water
15. Am ... habe ich bei Ihnen eine Bestellung aufgegeben. > On ... I __________ an order with you.
16. wir waren früher gute Freunde > we ________ to be good friends
17. von Anfang bis Ende > from start to __________
18. Es gab einen Unfall. > There has _______ an accident.
19. Bücher aus zweiter Hand > second-hand _________
20. nur noch 3 Minuten > _______ 3 minutes left

TEST 17

Was passt zusammen? Bilden Sie Sprichwörter oder Redensarten.

1.	Do not throw pearls	a)	before they hatch.
2.	Don't count your chickens	b)	before swine.
3.	Easy come,	c)	easy go.
4.	Faith will	d)	first served.
5.	First come,	e)	flies than vinegar.
6.	Fish and wine	f)	go together.
7.	Four eyes see	g)	laughs longest.
8.	God helps those	h)	more than two.
9.	He who laughs last,	i)	move mountains.
10.	Honey catches more	j)	who help themselves.

11.	Honour to whom	a)	but great ones escape.
12.	If you grease well,	b)	God disposes.
13.	In the country of the blind,	c)	honour is due.
14.	It is better to give	d)	is blind.
15.	Knowledge	e)	is power.
16.	Lies have	f)	short legs.
17.	Little thieves are hanged,	g)	than to receive.
18.	Love	h)	the one-eyed man is king.
19.	Lucky at cards,	i)	unlucky in love.
20.	Man proposes,	j)	you speed well.

TEST 18

Setzen Sie die Buchstaben in die richtige Reihenfolge, um die logische Entsprechung zu finden.

1. present : packaging = letter : [oeenvelp] envelope
2. pudding : eat = air : [haretbe] ______________
3. pullover : wool = belt : [eetrlha] ______________
4. rain : wet = towel : [ryd] ______________
5. Rhine : Germany = Nile : [gptyE] ______________
6. rich : poor = millionaire : [ergbga] ______________
7. ring : gold = tyre : [rbuerb] ______________
8. robber : rob = thief : [atles] ______________
9. rocks : pebbles = water : [rposd] ______________
10. Rome : Italy = Vienna : [iutaAsr] ______________
11. room : chairs = bus : [etsas] ______________
12. rose : flower = nightingale : [dibr] ______________
13. Russia : Russian = France : [hnrFec] ______________
14. safety : danger = safe : [urgaodesn] ______________
15. sandals : sunshine = Wellington boots : [anir] ______________
16. Easter rabbit : Easter = Santa Claus : [hCirtsasm] ______________
17. sausage : butcher = bread : [earkb] ______________
18. wrong : right = lie : [trhtu] ______________
19. script : alphabets = music : [oents] ______________
20. sea : coast = picture : [mrfea] ______________

TEST 19

Setzen Sie ein.

car children ~~comfort~~ electricity exchange feel fits learn lose Look milk name pass profession sign Sit table than today trust

1. das ist kein Trost für mich > that's no comfort_______ to me
2. den Verstand verlieren > to _______ one's mind
3. Vertrauen haben zu > to have confidence in / to _________
4. Setzen Sie sich! > _____ down!
5. die Milch ist sauer > the _______ has spoilt
6. Wie hoch ist der Wechselkurs? > What is the ______________ rate?
7. Sieh mich an! > _______ at me!
8. dieser Anzug sitzt gut > this suit _______ well
9. ein Zeichen geben > to make a _______
10. eine Prüfung bestehen > to _______ an examination
11. einen Beruf ausüben > to practise a _________________
12. Wir müssen Strom sparen. > We must conserve ___________________.
13. alle Kinder > all the ______________
14. Notieren Sie Ihren Namen und Ihre Adresse. > Write down your _______ and address.
15. er ist zwanzig Jahre jünger als ich > he is twenty years younger _______ me
16. heute ist Donnerstag > _________ is Thursday
17. Ist der Wagen versichert? > Is the _____ insured?
18. auf den Tisch stellen > to put on the _________
19. Lust haben zu > to __________ like
20. auswendig lernen > to _________ by heart

TEST 20

Was passt links und rechts zusammen?

1.	chin	pope
2.	church	thunder
3.	lightning	glass
4.	wine	petrol
5.	car	beard

a.	shirt	cloud
b.	sports	letters
c.	sky	collar
d.	music	notes
e.	word	Olympics

I.	tree	answer
II.	face	verdict
III.	question	nose
IV.	judge	wood
V.	cause	effect

A.	heater	rent
B.	plant	elections
C.	money	wallet
D.	apartment	warmth
E.	parties	leaf

TEST 21

Finden Sie waagerecht oder senkrecht 24 Körperteile.

z	b	d	c	e	h	n	t	s	s	m	h	h
e	e	c	t	y	c	q	h	h	t	o	b	a
c	a	h	h	e	a	x	u	o	o	u	o	n
h	r	i	r	b	b	t	m	u	m	t	s	d
e	d	n	o	r	t	f	b	l	a	h	o	s
e	b	f	a	o	z	z	h	d	c	b	m	h
k	r	f	t	w	b	o	n	e	h	f	m	j
p	e	a	**f**	**i**	**n**	**g**	**e**	**r**	**n**	**a**	**i**	**l**
p	a	c	o	z	t	o	n	g	u	e	t	d
x	s	e	n	o	s	e	e	s	h	s	o	x
e	t	f	i	n	g	e	r	k	s	r	o	q
w	p	n	e	c	k	h	a	i	r	s	t	l
m	h	h	e	a	d	p	k	n	e	e	h	l

TEST 22

Setzen Sie ein.

about about care glad hand ~~here~~ home less long manners morning or please radio tell turn voice were whenever yesterday

1. Darf ich hier parken? > Can I park here?
2. über kurz oder lang / früher oder später > sooner ____ later
3. ich bin an der Reihe / ich bin dran > it's my _______
4. das ist mir egal > I don't _______
5. jedesmal, wenn > ______________
6. mehr oder weniger > more or _______
7. es gehört sich nicht > it is bad ________
8. gestern morgen > ________________ morning
9. offen gestanden > to _______ the truth
10. sich sorgen um > to be uneasy / to worry _________
11. Die Badezimmer waren unhygienisch. > The bathrooms _______ not clean.
12. mit leiser Stimme > in a low _________
13. Bitte einen Tisch für 2 Personen. > A table for two, __________.
14. im Radio hören > to hear on the _________
15. in der Hand halten > to hold in one's _______
16. von früh bis spät > from ____________ till night
17. es ist mir lieb, dass > I am _______ that
18. etwa zehn Jahre > _________ 10 years
19. zu Hause sein > to be at _______
20. Auf Wiedersehen! / Bis bald! > Good-bye! / So _______! / See you (again)!

TEST 23

Setzen Sie die Buchstaben in die richtige Reihenfolge, um die gegenteilige Bedeutung zu finden.

1. to give - to [aekt] take
2. to accept - to [ueefrs] ____________________
3. to freeze - to [teml] ____________________
4. to push - to [lulp] ____________________
5. to approve - to [eoipapsvrd] ____________________
6. to lock - to [onklcu] ____________________
7. to succeed - to [alfi] ____________________
8. to appear - to [aaiprdpse] ____________________
9. to lend - to [rworob] ____________________
10. to ascend - to [ncedsde] ____________________
11. to search - to [dinf] ____________________
12. to trust - to [iuttrssd] ____________________
13. to break - to [ifx] ____________________
14. to halve - to [beolud] ____________________
15. to forget - to [berermme] ____________________
16. to agree - to [reiasdge] ____________________
17. to tie - to [inteu] ____________________
18. to behave - to [hvibsemea] ____________________
19. to throw - to [tachc] ____________________
20. to follow - to [dela] ____________________

TEST 24

Setzen Sie europäische Länder ein.
Welches Land ergibt sich in der senkrechten Reihe? (The ...)

						S	P									
								S	W		D		N			
												R	K			
												N	G		R	
						S	L		V		N					
												S	S			
									S			V		K		
				P		R	T		G		L					
						R		M								
S	W		T	Z		R	L		N							
								G			L		V			

TEST 25

Setzen Sie ein.

case cook day glasses hands history matter May ~~plastic~~ raining razor run sharp slow stroke Summer taste temperature thing Where

1. Kann ich eine Plastiktüte haben? > May I have a plastic bag?
2. das Essen kochen > to _______ / to prepare the meal
3. Was für ein Glück! > What a __________ of luck!
4. das schadet nichts > that does not __________
5. Hat man je so was gesehen? > Did you ever see such a ________?
6. Ich habe meine Brille zerbrochen. > I have broken my ____________.
7. Ich möchte mir die Hände waschen. > I want to wash my ________.
8. Mein Wagen hat kein Benzin mehr. > My car has ____ out of gas.
9. Der Sommer ist vorbei. > __________ is over.
10. Geschichte studieren > to study ____________
11. die Uhr geht fünf Minuten nach > the clock is five minutes _____
12. Sie hatte hohe Temperatur / hohes Fieber. > She had a high ________.
13. Wie schmeckt's? > How does it _________?
14. am Tag vorher / tags zuvor > the _____ before
15. Wo ist die nächste Werkstatt? > _________ is the next repair service / garage?
16. Es regnete, deshalb konnten wir nicht rausgehen. > It was __________ so we couldn't go out.
17. Steckdose für den Rasierapparat > socket for the ______
18. Dürfen wir ein Feuer anmachen? > _____ we light a fire?
19. auf jeden Fall > in any _______ / at any rate
20. Punkt 5 Uhr > at 5 o'clock _________

TEST 26

Finden Sie die logische Entsprechung.

conductor cutlery darkness dead glass glass hard heater Indonesia peace person police red referee roar ~~stage~~ temperature uniform white write

1. cinema : screen = theatre : stage
2. class : teacher = orchestra : ____________________
3. hospital : ill = graveyard : ____________________
4. clock : time = thermometer : ____________________
5. clown : costume = soldier : ____________________
6. cock : to crow = lion : to ____________________
7. oil : black = milk : ____________________
8. coffee : cup = wine : ____________________
9. cold : air conditioner = warm : ____________________
10. composer : to compose = author : to ____________________
11. court : judge = football game : ____________________
12. fire : fire brigade = crime : ____________________
13. cucumber : green = tomato : ____________________
14. cup : crockery = fork : ____________________
15. cupboard : wood = window pane : ____________________
16. cushion : soft = concrete : ____________________
17. damage : car = wound : ____________________
18. danger : safety = war : ____________________
19. day : light = night : ____________________
20. Delhi : India = Jakarta : ____________________

TEST 27

Kreuzworträtsel

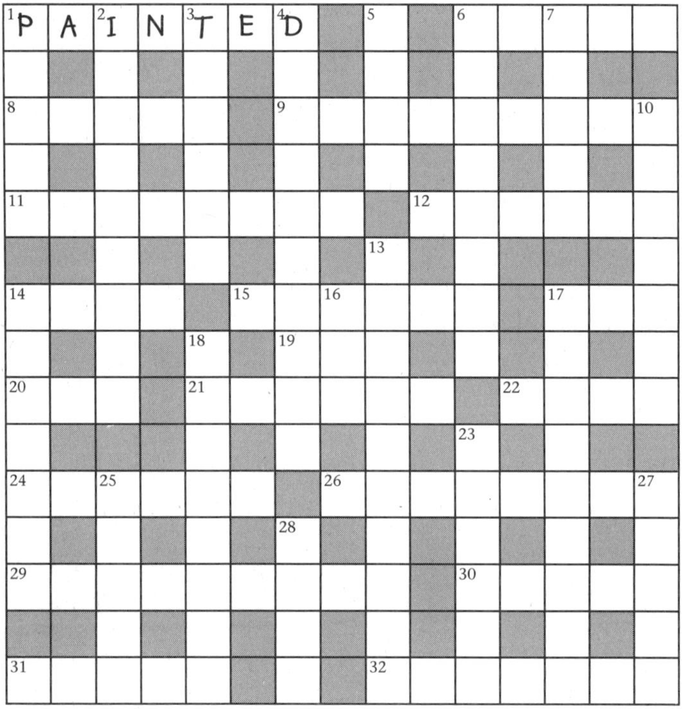

WAAGERECHT

1 He p****** the fence a bright red.

6 I t**** to call you, but you weren't home.

8 They made him a tempting o****.

9 We manufacture these products in our own f********.

11 He's d******* and isn't allowed to eat sweets.

12 The a***** patient was breathless and needed oxygen.

14 The s*** will dock tomorrow.

15 The Last S***** is a famous painting.

17 He drove a** the way.

19 Keep a stiff upper l**!

20 The driver of the v** was friendly.

21 Tell me as soon as he e***** the office.

22 The pubs b*** their own beer.

24 My niece and n***** are visiting me.

26 Did you like the sound of the b******* in Scotland?

29 Don't brush your hair with that dirty h********.

30 Please l**** me alone!

31 Please e**** all the data in the computer.

32 I want icecream for d*****

SENKRECHT

1 She's as p**** as a peacock.

2 The prices have gone up due to i********.

3 They ate t***** at Thanksgiving dinner.

4 He had no d********* in solving the puzzle.

5 The d*** of the ship was crowded.

6 He looks good in those t*******.

7 Very few I**** still speak Gaelic.

10 Don't s****** without chewing your food.

13 She a********* me with a request.

14 I'm in s****** heaven when I eat chocolate.

16 He loves apple p** with ice cream.

17 Look at that a******** flying high in the air!

18 I can't r******* his name.

23 This pie is made with a*****.

25 I can't read the small p**** in this book.

27 He whispered s**** nothings in her ear.

28 She talks too m***.

TEST 28

Setzen Sie ein.

better do drive enough hardly health not quarter ~~reason~~ rule there times tomorrow touch turn walk well with would younger

1. eben deswegen > for that very reason
2. ich bin es leid / ich habe genug davon > I have had _______ of it
3. ich möchte lieber > I _________ rather
4. rechts fahren > to _________ on the right
5. mein jüngerer Bruder > my _____________ brother
6. seine Schularbeiten / Hausaufgaben machen > to ____ one's homework
7. jemandem böse sein > to be angry _______ someone
8. gesund sein > to be in good ___________
9. sich wohl fühlen > to be _______
10. ein paarmal > several _________
11. eine Viertelstunde > a _____________ of an hour
12. einen Spaziergang machen > to go for a _______
13. sie macht kaum Fehler > she _________ makes any mistakes
14. um die Ecke biegen > to _______ the corner
15. in der Regel > as a _______
16. von sich hören lassen > to keep in _______
17. morgen früh > _______________ morning
18. erst morgen > _____ until tomorrow
19. es ist nicht nötig > _________ is no need
20. etwas Besseres > something ___________

TEST 29

Welches Wort passt in die logische Reihe?

1. spring, summer, _________, winter
2. May, June, _________, August
3. one, three, five, ___________
4. __________, Friday, Saturday, Sunday
5. the sun, the moon and the __________
6. January, _________, March, April
7. two, ________, six, eight
8. right, left, forward, ____________
9. Monday, Tuesday, __________, Thursday
10. first, second, __________, fourth
11. yesterday, ________, tomorrow, the day after tomorrow
12. always, often, seldom, _________
13. North, __________, East, West
14. past, present, ______________
15. in front, at the back / rear, __________, below

TEST 30

Kreuzworträtsel

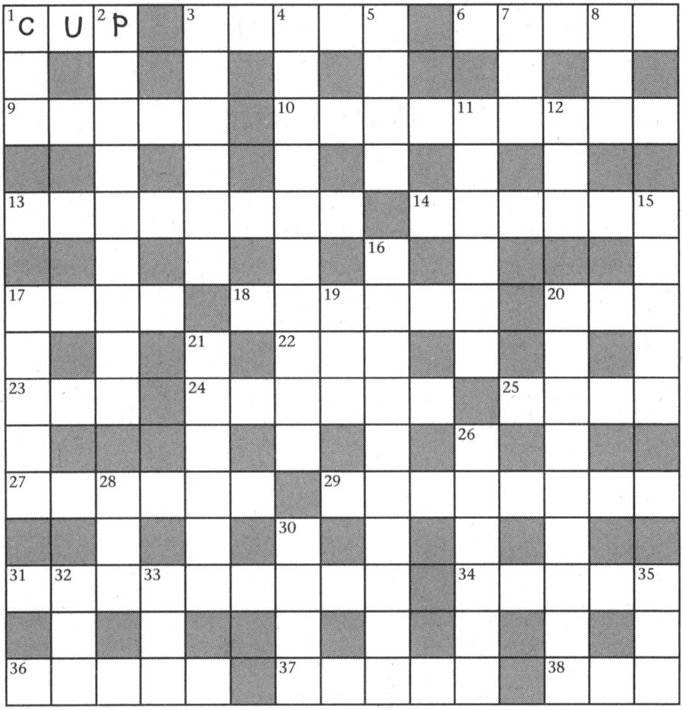

WAAGERECHT

1 She broke the tea c**.

3 I gave a b**** summary of what happened.

6 He is a famous a**** at the national theatre.

9 The river R**** flows through Europe.

10 A car is the only means of t******** here.

13 This book is from the b******* near my house.

14 That's the p***** who married them.

17 Does the timing s*** you?

18 We're visiting the national m***** today.

20 She doesn't look her a**.

22 She c** swim very fast.

23 He had e** and rolls for breakfast.

24 She's so p*****, she doesn't need make-up.

25 She's isn't a*** to come.

27 P***** borders on Germany.

29 You'll need an u******* if it rains.

31 I have an i******** meeting this morning.

34 The office is on the n**** floor.

36 He bought himself a Swiss army k****.

37 There are policemen at e**** corner.

38 He's pierced his left e**.

SENKRECHT

1 My c** is in the garage.

2 She is suffering from food p********.

3 She has cancer in her right b*****.

4 I was i********* to my new colleagues.

5 My f*** has 3 rooms.

7 Wear a c** if you're playing in the sun.

8 We left o** house early.

11 S***** is my favourite seafood.

12 You o** me a lot of money.

15 Don't keep running here and t****!

16 She's one c********* taller than me.

17 The baby was tired and went to s****.

19 He s** on his mother's lap.

20 We need an a******** to take him to hospital.

21 I need a bottle o***** to open the bottles.

26 He drank a glass of b***** to help his cold.

28 She bit her l** in agitation.

30 H*** you heard the news?

32 M** aren't as perceptive as women.

33 Switch o** the music!

35 She knows h** own weaknesses.

TEST 31

Setzen Sie ein.

car charge coming damage dog door drink God Good hospital machine Make Noon No performance ~~salt~~ sea shoes surprise too

1. Das Salz kommt aus dem Toten Meer. > This _salt_ comes from the Dead Sea.
2. Fasse dich kurz! > _______ it short!
3. Ich komme gleich! > I'm just __________!
4. Schaden anrichten > to do harm / to cause __________
5. Beginn der Vorstellung um ... > The _______________ begins at ...
6. Wein trinken > to ________ wine
7. Ihr Wagen behindert den Verkehr. > Your _____ is holding up the traffic.
8. Die Maschine verbraucht zuviel Strom. > This ____________ uses too much electricity.
9. Sie müssen ins Krankenhaus. > You must go to the _____________.
10. Hiermit stellen wir Ihnen folgende Beträge in Rechnung ... > We herewith _______ you the following ...
11. Einfahrt verboten! > ____ entry!
12. übers Meer segeln > to sail across the _____
13. Mittag ist die heißeste Tageszeit. > _______ is the hottest part of the day.
14. Bitte putzen Sie meine Schuhe. > Please clean my ________.
15. Um Himmels willen! > _______ heavens!
16. an die Tür klopfen > to knock at the _______
17. Der Hund bellt. > The _____ is barking.
18. Gott sei Dank! > Thank _____! / Fortunately!
19. zu meiner Überraschung > to my ______________
20. Würden Sie auch den Ölstand nachprüfen? > Could you check the oil, _____?

TEST 32

Finden Sie die logische Entsprechung.

beautiful boss ~~crocodile~~ day deep drink Dutch fleet fork head hiss lie oil reap round shampoo summer twelve verse water

1. sea : shark = river : crocodile
2. second : minute = hour : ______
3. fish : school = ship : ______
4. shoe : foot = hat : ______
5. six : three = twenty four : ______
6. skin : soap = hair : ______
7. skyscraper : tall = well : ______
8. lion : to roar = snake : to ______
9. snow : winter = sunshine : ______
10. sofa : to sit = bed : to ______
11. soldier : general = secretary : ______
12. solid : liquid = ice : ______
13. poem : stanza = song : ______
14. soup : spoon = cake : ______
15. South Africa : diamonds = Saudi Arabia : ______
16. Spain : Spanish = Holland : ______
17. spider : ugly = butterfly : ______
18. plate : to eat = glass : to ______
19. spring : to sow = autumn : to ______
20. square : angular = circle : ______

TEST 33

Setzen Sie die fehlenden Vokale „a“, „e“, „o“ ein, um den Witz zu verstehen.

A man has _ s_us_g_ st_nd dir_ctly _pp_sit_ _ b_nk.

_n _ld fri_nd c_m_s _nd _sks him:

„C_n y_u l_nd m_ s_m_ m_n_y?“

„I’m s_rry, I c_n’t!“

„_nd why n_t?“

„B_c_us_ I h_v_ _ c_ntr_ct with th_ b_nk!“

„Wh_t kind _f _ c_ntr_ct?“

„I d_n’t l_nd _ny m_n_y _nd th_y d_n’t s_ll _ny s_us_g_s!“

TEST 34

Setzen Sie ein.

advance age back bread carry coat cross fact going mistake need nowhere people question same something something ~~south~~ until watch

1. ich fahre nach Süden > I'm travelling south
2. das führt zu nichts > that leads ____________
3. ich bin gleich wieder da > I'll be _______ shortly / in a bit
4. ich muss weggehen > I must be off / I must be _________
5. meine Uhr geht vor > my _________ is fast
6. etwas stimmt nicht > ______________ is wrong
7. den Mantel anziehen > to put on one's _______
8. die Grenze überschreiten > to _________ the border / frontier
9. die meisten Leute > most __________
10. ein Stück Brot > a piece of _________
11. eine Frage stellen > to ask a ______________
12. eine schwere Last tragen > to _________ a heavy load
13. wir sind gleich alt > we are the _______ age
14. im Voraus > in ____________
15. in der Tat > in ________
16. er ist in meinem Alter > he is my _____
17. erst morgen > not _________ tomorrow
18. es ist nicht nötig > there is no _______
19. etwas Gutes > ________________ good
20. aus Versehen > by ____________

TEST 35

Setzen Sie die Buchstaben in die richtige Reihenfolge, um die logische Entsprechung zu finden.

1. Germany : German = Denmark : [iahnsD] Danish
2. desert : sand = sea : [eawrt] ____________
3. dog : animal = flower : [lnpta] ____________
4. dog : to bark = cat : [to emw] ____________
5. eagle : to fly = whale : [to mwis] ____________
6. early : late = breakfast : [rniden] ____________
7. elephant : big = mouse : [lmlsa] ____________
8. elephant : trunk = human : [oesn] ____________
9. child : pocket money = employee : [aayslr] ____________
10. England : monarchy = France : [lecubirp] ____________
11. evening : time of the day = autumn : [nseosa] ____________
12. expressionism : painting = baroque : [hcuretericta] ____________
13. eye : blind = ear : [efad] ____________
14. eye : to see = ear : [to erah] ____________
15. fan : heat = heating : [odlc] ____________
16. far : near = distance : [reesansn] ____________
17. to gain weight : to lose weight = fat : [hnti] ____________
18. father : daughter = king : [renscisp] ____________

TEST 36

Setzen Sie die Buchstaben in die richtige Reihenfolge, um die gegenteilige Bedeutung zu finden.

1. direct - [neitircd] indirect
2. perfect - [fmcerepti] ____________
3. loose - [higtt] ____________
4. together - [eaeaprst] ____________
5. yesterday - [wrooromt] ____________
6. flexible - [bxelniflie] ____________
7. liquid - [oidls] ____________
8. now - [eatrl] ____________
9. offensive - [eesvindfe] ____________
10. noisy - [eutqi] ____________
11. scarce - [tnbaduan] ____________
12. arid - [telfrei] ____________
13. tolerant - [ateonlinrt] ____________
14. spicy - [lndba] ____________
15. arrogant - [uebhml] ____________
16. plausible - [iulmliepasb] ____________
17. shortsighted - [hgeiotslngd] ____________
18. strong - [kewa] ____________

TEST 37

Setzen Sie ein.

another ago ~~any~~ back coffee great hundreds meet nationality over page park parking road seriously skidded Take That would Welcome

1. Haben Sie Zigaretten? > Have you got __any__ cigarettes?
2. Das ist ja großartig! > It's simply ________!
3. Lassen Sie sich Zeit! > _______ your time!
4. Ich möchte ein Einzelzimmer mit Dusche. > I ________ like a single room with a shower.
5. Seien Sie willkommen! > ____________!
6. seinen Wagen parken > to _______ one's car
7. Möchten Sie noch eine Tasse Tee? > Would you like ________ cup of tea?
8. Die Sache ist erledigt! > _______ settles the matter!
9. Ihr Auto rutschte auf der vereisten Straße. > Her car ________ on the icy road.
10. Wann werden wir uns wieder treffen? > When shall we _______ again?
11. Niemand ist ernstlich verletzt. > Nobody is _____________ hurt.
12. Bitte wenden! > Please turn _______!
13. In dieser Straße gibt es Parkuhren. > There are ____________ meters in this street.
14. unten auf der Seite > at the bottom of the _______
15. vor einiger Zeit > some time _____
16. Er ist deutscher Nationalität. > His _______________ is German.
17. rückwärts fahren > to _______ up / to reverse
18. Führt diese Straße direkt in die Stadt? > Does this _______ lead straight into the city?
19. jemand zum Kaffee einladen > to invite someone for a cup of _____
20. Hunderte von > ______________ of

TEST 38

Welche Körperteile sind gemeint?

1. to hug someone: arms
2. to chew food: ______
3. to think: ______
4. to kiss someone: ______
5. to hit someone hard: ______
6. to smell: ______
7. to see: ______
8. to hear: ______
9. to taste: ______
10. it beats: ______
11. to clap: ______
12. to point: ______
13. to feel: ______
14. you get it cut at the barber's: ______
15. you shave it: ______
16. you wear a necklace around it: ______
17. to breathe: ______
18. to show one's strength: ______
19. to tap it to music: ______
20. to run fast: ______

Kreuzworträtsel

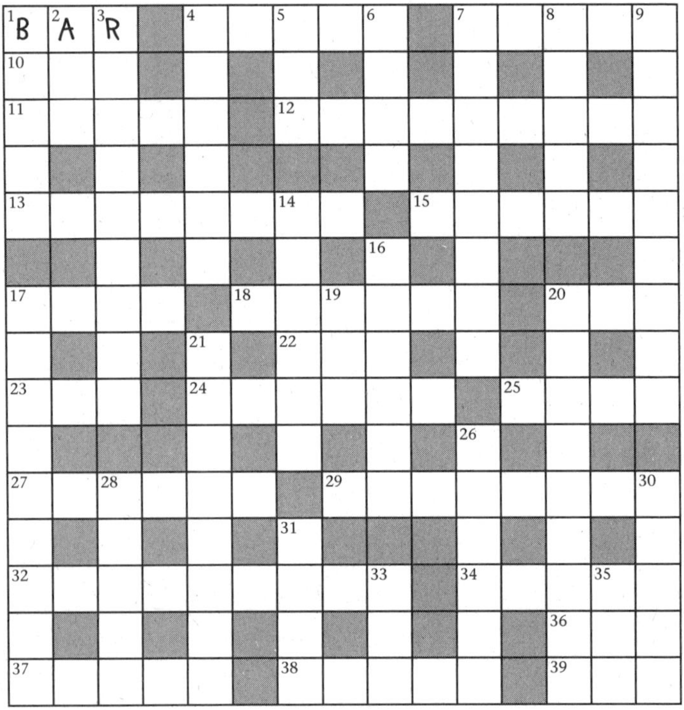

WAAGERECHT

1 Let's have a drink at the b**.

4 Surfing is a s****.

7 This cycle didn't cost me much, it was c****.

10 He's very active despite his a**.

11 Have you tried the l**** beer?

12 Could you t******** this English document into French?

13 S******* the white clothes from the coloured ones.

15 I'd like a b***** of water, please

17 China is in A***.

18 Is a***** there?

20 The wine is in an old v**.

22 Can you g** me a coke?

23 Don't write with that p**.
24 My aunt's son is my c***** .
25 I love i*** soda.
27 Could you r***** my broken chair?
29 We bought pottery from the c******* shop.
32 I need a g******** to help me tour the city.
34 I'd like a glass of fresh g**** juice.
36 Do wear a t** for the interview!
37 The dessert is too s****.
38 Could I have a d**** to dry my hair?
39 The e** of the movie was disappointing.

SENKRECHT

1 He's juggling with multi-coloured b****.
2 I finished the work long a**.
3 Check in at the hotel r******** .
4 Your s***** will be raised this month.
5 Get o** of my house!
6 I want our t*** to win the match.
7 Be courteous to every c******* in the shop.
8 What is the e**** time of departure?
9 The rain p******** us from playing the match.
14 We're having ox t***** soup today.
16 I didn't see the n***** about the meeting.
17 He loves a******** soup.
19 Y**, I would like that.
20 Did you v******** her for polio?
21 The driver died in the a*******.
26 The boy is in d***** of drowning in the river.
28 She won the first p**** in the competition.
30 It's unsafe to drive at a high s**** in the rain.
31 She ate her f*** slowly.
33 Where is the car k**?
35 I need a hair p** for my hair.

TEST 40

Setzen Sie ein.

aches ~~bad~~ coat else else funny height hungry nothing on ought Our pay rate rising side thirteen tomorrow understand weather

1. das ist nicht so schlimm > it's not as bad as all that
2. ich bin hungrig / ich habe Hunger > I'm ________
3. ich sollte eigentlich arbeiten > I ________ to work
4. bei schönem Wetter > when the ____________ is fine
5. der Kopf tut mir weh > my head ________
6. Verstehen Sie deutsch? > Do you _________________ German?
7. die Sonne geht auf > the sun is __________
8. Wie hoch ist der Wechselkurs? > What is the exchange _______?
9. ein komischer Einfall > a ________ idea
10. eine Strafe zahlen > to _____ a fine
11. einen Mantel tragen > to wear a _______
12. Wir sind 2 Erwachsene und 4 Kinder. > _____ party consists of 2 adults and 4 children.
13. wir sind gleich groß > we are the same ________
14. alles andere > everything _______
15. im zweiten Stock wohnen > to live ___ the second floor
16. dreizehn Meter lang > ______________ metres long
17. Ich fahre morgen ab > I'm leaving ______________
18. es ist nichts übriggeblieben > there is ____________ left
19. etwas anderes > something _______
20. auf der rechten Seite > on the right / on the right hand _______

TEST 41

Setzen Sie das richtige Fragewort ein.

How How How How Since Till What What What What When Where Where Where Which ~~Who~~ Who Whom Whose Why

1. Who is that? - That is my boss.
2. _______ do you come from? - From Switzerland.
3. _______ do you live? - In Paris.
4. _______ does that cost? - Only a few dollars.
5. _______ are you calling up? - My parents.
6. _______ are you lending the book to? - To my friend.
7. _______ many children do you have? - A boy and a girl.
8. _______ wallet is that? - It is mine.
9. _______ actor do you like best? - Charlie Chaplin.
10. _______ often do you have class? - Twice a week.
11. _______ long does the journey take? - Six hours.
12. _______ much time do you have? - 3 hours.
13. _______ did you get married? - 10 years ago.
14. _______ aren't you going to school? - Because I'm ill.
15. _______ are you travelling to? - To Madrid
16. _______ are you thinking of? - Of my work.
17. _______ do you use the computer for? - For e-mail.
18. _______ are you waiting for? - For the bus.
19. _______ when have you lived abroad? - Since 1998.
20. _______ when will you be here? - Till Monday.

TEST 42

Welches Wort passt nicht in die Reihe?

1. ~~sand~~ - sugar - salt - pepper
2. Denmark - Sweden - Finland - Greece
3. lid - cork - roof - match
4. to stand - to jump - to spring - to climb
5. television - curtains - heater - sky
6. cucumber - carrots - fish - potatoes
7. dolphin - shark - herring - tuna
8. German - Bavarian - Italian - Polish
9. December - summer - autumn - winter
10. fly - mosquito - goat - bee
11. floppy - monitor - printer - pencil
12. Europe - Austria - Switzerland - Poland
13. can opener - pot - corkscrew - bottle opener
14. friendly - dumb - stingy - intolerant
15. duck - spider - turkey - goose
16. figs - cherries - kiwis - tomatoes
17. window - book - wall - floor
18. finger - hand - thumb - face
19. grey - strong - green - purple
20. belt - trouser - hat - suspenders

TEST 43

Setzen Sie ein.

by car corner ~~declare~~ excludes faithful give judge latest need night no other present sauna sick television try outdoors worry

1. Haben Sie etwas zu verzollen? > Do you have anything to declare?
2. nach der neuesten Mode > according to the __________ fashion
3. Ich gebe Ihnen eine Spritze. > I'm going to _______ you an injection.
4. Ich möchte einen Wagen mieten. > I would like to rent a _____.
5. schlafen gehen / zu Bett gehen > to retire for the ________ / to go to bed
6. Unsere Kinder spielen gern draußen. > Our children like to play ________.
7. jemandem treu bleiben > to remain ____________ to somebody
8. Der Elektriker hat unseren Fernseher repariert. > The electrician repaired our _________________.
9. Beurteile Menschen nicht nach dem Äußeren. > Don't ________ people by appearances.
10. sich Sorgen / Gedanken machen über > to __________ about
11. Die Transportkosten sind nicht im Angebot enthalten. > The offer ______________ transportation costs.
12. sie lieben sich > they love each _________
13. mir ist schlecht / übel > I feel ill / I feel _______
14. in die Ecke stellen > to put in the __________
15. unter keinen Umständen / auf gar keinen Fall > on ____ account
16. mit Gewalt > ______ force
17. Er wird sein Bestes versuchen. > He'll ____ his best.
18. Brauchen Sie ein Einzel- oder Doppelzimmer? > Do you _______ a single or a double room?
19. Ist eine Sauna vorhanden? > Do you have _________ facilities?
20. anwesend sein > to be ____________

TEST 44

Finden Sie die logische Entsprechung.

believe close defence departure divide dog dry familiar finish head lazy ~~mayor~~ patient rocket sing sweet Scandinavia Spain university visitors

1. state : president = city : mayor
2. Stockholm : Sweden = Madrid : ____________
3. stocking : foot = cap : ____________
4. story : to tell = song : to ____________
5. stranger : friend = alien : ____________
6. underground train : passengers = zoo : ____________
7. salt : salty = sugar : ____________
8. sure : unsure = to know : to ____________
9. swamp : humid = desert : ____________
10. Panama : Central America = Sweden : ____________
11. taxi driver : taxi = astronaut : ____________
12. teacher : school = professor : ____________
13. teacher : student = doctor : ____________
14. television : to switch off = window : to ____________
15. thin : fat = industrious : ____________
16. tiger : cat = wolf : ____________
17. to add : to subtract = to multiply : to ____________
18. to arrive : to depart = arrival : ____________
19. to attack : to defend = attack : ____________
20. to fall asleep : to wake up = to begin : to ____________

TEST 45

Setzen Sie die Buchstaben in die richtige Reihenfolge, um die logische Entsprechung zu finden.

1. fence : wood = wall : [ntose] stone
2. finger : ring = neck : [eakelccn] ____________
3. fire : ashes = cause : [etfcfe] ____________
4. fish : aquarium = cow : [narb] ____________
5. fish : gills = man : [ugsnl] ____________
6. fisherman : net = hunter : [ung] ____________
7. fishing rod : to fish = gun : [to ohtso] ____________
8. flour : bread = cocoa : [ltchcooae] ____________
9. flower : plant = fish : [nlmaai] ____________
10. foot : toe = hand : [irgfen] ____________
11. foreigner : visa = driver : [eciecnl] ____________
12. France : cognac = Russia : [okadv] ____________
13. frog : to jump = snake : to [lithsre] ____________
14. garbage : garbage can = cigarette : [hsrtaay] ____________
15. gardener : garden = cook : [cientkh] ____________
16. generous : thrifty = rich : [orpo] ____________
17. Germany : country = Berlin : [yitc] ____________
18. girl : boy = sister : [erthobr] ____________
19. glass : to break = bomb : [to xldoeep] ____________
20. gold : plastic = expensive : [hacpe] ____________

TEST 46

Setzen Sie ein.

beautiful bicycle doctor early garage Germany hour in masterpiece parking passed song stomach Speak task there third ~~trusted~~ tune What

1. Man kann ihm zum Glück vertrauen. > Fortunately, he can be trusted.
2. Parken verboten! > No ____________!
3. das Instrument stimmen > to _______ an instrument
4. Was fehlt Ihnen? > _______ is wrong with you?
5. den Arzt holen > to call in the __________
6. der/die/das Dritte > the _________
7. die deutsche Geschichte > the history of ____________
8. Sie hat die Prüfung bestanden / geschafft. > She ________ the examination.
9. Wie schön das ist! > How ________________!
10. ein Lied singen > to sing a _______
11. eine Aufgabe stellen > to set a _______
12. eine halbe Stunde > half an _______
13. am frühen Morgen / frühmorgens > _________ in the morning
14. Wo ist die nächste Autowerkstatt? > Where is the next __________?
15. Sprich lauter! > ________ up!
16. er hat ein Meisterwerk geschaffen > he has created a ___________________
17. erstens / an erster Stelle > ____ the first place
18. es ist niemand da > _________ is nobody there
19. etwas gegen Bauchweh > something for ____________ ache
20. aufs Rad steigen > to get on the ____________

TEST 47

Finden Sie waagerecht oder senkrecht 38 positive Eigenschaften.

h	e	l	p	f	u	l	v	e	p	o	j	h	p	h	u	h	a
b	a	l	a	n	c	e	d	l	r	v	o	a	u	u	p	o	c
p	a	t	i	e	n	t	e	e	e	e	l	r	n	m	l	n	t
p	o	l	i	t	e	z	w	g	t	r	l	d	c	o	o	e	i
t	o	l	e	r	a	n	t	a	t	s	y	w	t	r	c	s	v
p	r	q	u	i	e	t	z	n	y	a	n	o	u	o	h	t	e
l	e	b	r	a	v	e	y	t	v	t	i	r	a	u	e	h	a
d	**s**	**y**	**m**	**p**	**a**	**t**	**h**	**e**	**t**	**i**	**c**	k	l	s	e	m	k
j	p	c	b	s	o	c	i	a	b	l	e	i	l	t	r	d	p
l	o	v	i	n	g	x	l	e	a	e	z	n	e	h	f	c	c
m	n	o	p	t	i	m	i	s	t	i	c	g	g	i	u	h	v
b	s	b	e	a	u	t	i	f	u	l	e	f	u	n	l	a	w
h	i	n	v	a	r	e	l	i	a	b	l	e	v	c	j	r	s
c	b	e	l	i	n	t	e	l	l	i	g	e	n	t	i	m	t
j	l	a	q	v	a	t	h	l	e	t	i	c	y	f	a	i	r
d	e	t	x	f	r	a	t	t	r	a	c	t	i	v	e	n	o
e	x	c	i	t	i	n	g	f	r	i	e	n	d	l	y	g	n
c	l	e	a	n	g	e	n	e	r	o	u	s	r	i	c	h	g

TEST 48

Kreuzworträtsel

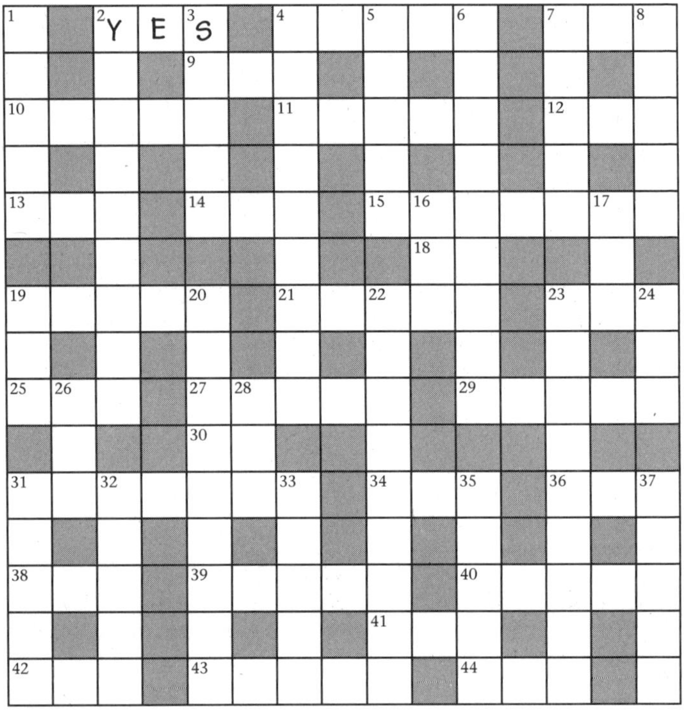

WAAGERECHT

2 Y**, I work here.
4 They went to the o**** instead of to the theatre.
7 I have one s** and one daughter.
9 My c** has run out of petrol.
10 Spaghetti and macaroni are types of p****.
11 The criminal was executed on the electric c****.
12 Would you like some i** in your drink?
13 Should I d** my grey hair black?
14 He hurt his left e** and can't see very well.
15 We're seeing a classical play at the t******.
18 I a* at home today.
19 The Taj Mahal is in I****.
21 T**** are my shoes, those are yours.
23 I'd like some bread a** butter.

25 What did you s**?
27 The letter needs a s**** before you post it.
29 He's t**** after all the hard work.
30 Could I speak t* him?
31 She has everything under c******.
34 The children a** playing outside.
36 I hope you like the green p** soup.
38 The a** in the city is polluted.
39 She'd like to l**** Spanish.
40 The t**** pulled into the railway station.
41 The girl screamed into his e**.
42 T** food here is delicious.
43 Go a**** with the plan.
44 He's turned grey with a**.

SENKRECHT

1 His motorcycle is faster than my m****.
2 Y******** she was fine, but today she's ill.
3 I need a s**** to measure the weight.
4 We listened to the Philharmonic O******** playing.
5 Could you tell us the e**** price?
6 They signed an a******** to divide the land.
7 a typewriter key: s****
8 Her n**** and nephew are visiting her.
16 He h** a lot of money and is very powerful.
17 We take the dogs for a r** every evening.
19 The cat is lying in i** basket.
20 A******** is the home of the kangaroo.
22 I understood after he e******** it to me.
23 He loves flying an a********.
24 What d** you do yesterday evening?
26 That was a long time a**.
28 I'd like some beer, t**.
31 The restaurants on the c**** serve fresh fish.
32 The n**** will give you an injection.
33 Do you have to l**** already?
35 Do you have any e**** sheets of paper?
37 Don't a**** me with your questions!

TEST 49

Setzen Sie ein.

advice break broken change ~~forward~~ Good if less light little make remember reserve school some soon thanks This would your

1. nach vorn > forward
2. ich erinnere mich, dass > I ______________ that
3. ich trinke lieber Wein als Bier > I _________ rather have wine than beer
4. schlimmstenfalls / im äußersten Fall > ____ the worst comes to the worst
5. Geld wechseln > to ___________ money
6. jemanden um Rat fragen > to ask someone's ___________
7. wenig Zeit > ___________ time
8. Der Schalter ist kaputt. > The switch is ___________.
9. sich den Arm brechen > to _________ one's arm
10. Biegen Sie nach der dritten Verkehrsampel rechts ab. > Turn to the right at the third traffic _________.
11. viel weniger > much _______
12. Dieser Mann ist verletzt. > _______ man is injured.
13. mit Dank annehmen > to accept with ___________
14. Viel Glück! > _______ luck!
15. glücklich machen > to _______ happy
16. immer der Nase nach > just follow _______ nose
17. in die Schule gehen > to go to ___________
18. so bald wie möglich > as _______ as possible
19. Bringen Sie mir bitte etwas Zitrone. > Can I have _______ lemon, please.
20. Es ist besser, eine Reservierung für die Tickets zu machen. > It is better to _________ the tickets.

TEST 50

Finden Sie Wortpaare mit gegenteiliger Bedeutung.

calm covered drab gigantic ~~horizontal~~ illegal masculine optimistic permanent spiritual stingy tame unknown

1. vertical - horizontal
2. boisterous - ____________
3. feminine - ____________
4. pessimistic - ____________
5. microscopic - ____________
6. famous - ____________
7. generous - ____________
8. colorful - ____________
9. wild - ____________
10. bare - ____________
11. legal - ____________
12. temporary - ____________
13. physical - ____________

TEST 51

Setzen Sie die Namen europäischer Länder ein.

TEST 52

Setzen Sie ein.

beach ~~cards~~ contact country doctor eggs enough Have left look lose matches once out outside quarrel repair spoilt Shut want

1. Karten spielen > to play cards
2. das genügt völlig > that's quite ___________
3. Was willst du eigentlich? > What do you _______ anyway?
4. Hat man je so was gesehen? > _____ you ever seen such a thing?
5. Ich habe meine Kontaktlinsen verloren. > I have lost my _____________ lenses.
6. Ich möchte zwei Rühreier. > I would like two scrambled _______.
7. Meine linke Hand blutet. > My _______ hand is bleeding.
8. den Streit beilegen > to settle a _____________
9. die Milch ist verdorben / sauer > the milk has ___________
10. Sie müssen in drei Monaten wieder ausreisen. > You must leave the __________ again in three months.
11. ein für allemal > _______ and for all
12. eine Schachtel Streichhölzer > a box of _____________
13. einen Kranken pflegen > to _______ after a patient
14. das Hotel am Strand. > the hotel on the _________.
15. draußen geht ein Wind > there is a strong wind blowing _____________
16. arbeitslos sein > to be _____ of work
17. Tür zu! / Bitte die Tür schließen! > _______ the door, please!
18. Würden Sie das Auto reparieren? > Could you ___________ the car?
19. Rufen Sie einen Arzt. > Call a ___________.
20. aus den Augen verlieren > to _______ sight of

TEST 53

Setzen Sie die Sätze in die richtige Reihenfolge.

○ „But now I can't get it out of my head!"

○ „Beware! If you think of noodle soup while you are digging, you won't find it."

○ „Damn! I've never thought of noodle soup in my life!"

○ „You'll find the treasure a few metres under the ground."

○ „Take a spade with you and dig for treasure."

○ „Wait for a clear night with a full moon and go to the old graveyard at midnight."

○ „You will be very rich if you do exactly as I tell you."

○ On a clear night with a full moon he goes to the graveyard and begins to dig.

(1) Peter goes to a fortune teller to ask about his future.

○ Peter is excited about the treasure and buys himself a spade.

○ She looks into a crystal ball for a long time and then tells him:

○ Suddenly he throws down the spade and runs away:

TEST 54

Setzen Sie die Buchstaben in die richtige Reihenfolge, um die logische Entsprechung zu finden.

1. good : bad = advantage : [avneiadsdgat] disadvantage
2. good luck : bad luck = success : [ralfieu] ____________
3. gorilla : jungle = camel : [teersd] ____________
4. grapefruit : bitter = vinegar : [orsu] ____________
5. green : go = red : [ptos] ____________
6. group : individual = together : [nloea] ____________
7. guitar : trumpet = to strum : [to lwob] ____________
8. gun : bullet = bow : [orawr] ____________
9. hammer : nail = screwdriver : [ecswr] ____________
10. hand : glove = foot : [ehso] ____________
11. hands : to stroke = lips : [to isks] ____________
12. happiness : to laugh = unhappiness : [to ryc] ____________
13. head : heart = reason : [smotonie] ____________
14. hearing aid : to hear = spectacles : [to ese] ____________
15. heaven : hell = angel : [iedlv] ____________
16. Helsinki : Finland = Dublin : [lrnedaI] ____________
17. train : conductor = aeroplane : [eswsaesdtr] ____________
18. house : homeless = work : [yndlmeoupe] ____________

TEST 55

Setzen Sie ein.

banks best black cold else faintest fault first for from ~~May~~
of right same soul teeth these two welcome worse

1. Darf ich die Rechnung haben? > May I have the check?
2. ich friere / mich friert / mir ist kalt > I am ________
3. ich tu's trotzdem > I'll do it all the ________
4. schwarz auf weiß > in __________ and white
5. keiner von beiden > neither of the ______
6. sich die Zähne putzen > to brush one's __________
7. ich habe nicht die geringste Ahnung > I haven't got the __________ idea
8. willkommen heißen > to ______________
9. mit Leib und Seele > with heart and ________
10. Bitte bügeln Sie diese Anziehsachen / Kleidungsstücke. > Please iron __________ clothes.
11. immer schlechter > __________ and worse / from bad to worse
12. in diesem Augenblick > at the moment / ________ now
13. An wem liegt es? / Wer ist schuld? > Whose __________ is it?
14. golden / aus Gold > golden / made ____ gold
15. aus Deutschland > ________ Germany
16. sonst nichts > nothing ________
17. er tut sein Bestes > he does his ________
18. erstens / an erster Stelle > in the __________ place
19. das Ufer der Themse > the __________ of the River Thames
20. etwas gegen starke Zahnschmerzen > something ______ a bad toothache

TEST 56

Stimmt das?

1. Carbon is required for starting a fire. false
2. An emu is a bird. true
3. The Statue of Liberty is in New York. _________
4. Fish can live only in water. _________
5. The river Thames flows through London. _________
6. The heart has one valve. _________
7. Arabic is written from right to left. _________
8. Glass expands when heated. _________
9. Potatoes grow under the ground. _________
10. A rat is bigger than a mouse. _________
11. If you can't see things nearby you are short-sighted. _________
12. The Grand Canyon is in the eastern United States. _________
13. A leap year has three hundred sixty-six days. _________
14. French is not spoken in Canada. _________
15. America is named after Amerigo Vespucci. _________
16. Eighteen is a prime number. _________
17. The Mississippi is the broadest river in the world. _________
18. A cauliflower is a flower. _________
19. Mozart was a famous composer. _________
20. An ant is a big animal. _________

TEST 57

Kreuzworträtsel

WAAGERECHT

1 She loves listening to m****, especially jazz.
4 R** is the colour which denotes danger.
6 An a**** a day keeps the doctor away.
9 The i** on the lake is thick enough to skate on.
10 He put his a** around her.
11 The car won't start, something is wrong with the m****.
12 He's five years o**.
13 I s** your brother yesterday at the shopping centre.
15 Have you had enough, or would you like some m***?
16 An a***** is a type of nut.
18 Today is the 12** of July.
20 The h*** of the shoe came off.
21 W********* D.C. is the capital of the USA.

24 They did it by t*********, nobody helped them.
25 What is the exchange r*** of the dollar into the yen?
28 N*, I don't work here.
29 It's too hot to wear shoes, wear your s*****s.
31 She's a movie s***. She has acted in many films.
32 Please s** the carton down gently, it contains glass.
35 She was my classmate, but I don't know h** very well.
36 Would you like some French o**** soup?
37 I need not o**, but two new dresses.
38 He's blind in one e**, but can see well with the other.
39 W**** did you buy that from?
40 D** you meet him yesterday?
41 He drinks one l**** of juice a day.

SENKRECHT

1 'Sayonara' m**** 'Good bye' in Japanese.
2 The keys must be s********, but I can't find them!
3 Which movie is playing at the c***** tonight?
4 He's changed r********* since we met, I hardly know him.
5 I have a d*** with her at 8 p.m.
6 Eighteen people can fly in this a******* at a time.
7 The tourist took a p**** of the carvings.
8 Every e** marks a new beginning.
14 I a** pizza for lunch.
17 Can you d**** the tango?
19 He t********* to kill her son if she didn't comply.
20 She h**** him, but loves his brother.
22 We t******** the goods to the customer by ship.
23 How do you say 'breaded veal cutlet' in French? - E*******.
26 I got a blister on my right t** because of my new shoe.
27 She'd like to t***** all around the world.
30 He had the n**** to ask for a raise!
33 T**** are a lot of jobs vacant.
34 The windows are banging due to the w***.
35 Good morning, h** are you?

TEST 58

Setzen Sie ein.

battery ~~by~~ Cheer his holds limit lot luck minute Open or pace party recommended sample shop taste took understands vanilla

1. Fahren wir mit dem Zug oder Auto? > Shall we go _by_ train or car?
2. das kostet viel Geld > that will cost a ______ of money
3. Ich liebe Vanilleeis. > I love ______________ ice cream.
4. Schritt halten mit > to keep ________ with
5. der Saal fasst neunzig Personen > the hall __________ ninety people
6. Verkäuferin gesucht > ________ assistant wanted
7. Ihre Firma wurde uns durch ... empfohlen. > Your company was ______________________ to us by ... .
8. Die Batterie ist entladen. > The ______________ is weak.
9. Sie machte ein Foto von ihm. > She _________ a picture of him.
10. Wie heißt er doch gleich? > What's ______ name again?
11. Sie versteht sehr wenig Englisch. > She ______________________ very little English.
12. Hier öffnen! > ________ here!
13. Ein Muster finden Sie in der Anlage. > Please find enclosed a ____________.
14. Wir hatten eine schöne Geburtstagsfeier. > We had a nice birthday __________.
15. bitter schmecken > to ____________ bitter
16. alles hat seine Grenzen > there is a __________ to everything
17. Glück bringen > to bring good ________
18. Möchten Sie lieber eine Cola oder ein Bier? > Would you like a coke ____ a beer?
19. Kopf hoch! / Nur Mut! > __________ up!
20. auf die Minute > to the ____________

TEST 59

Finden Sie die logische Entsprechung.

air bedroom country guilt legs loud oral pages park pavement permission refuse river ~~sailor~~ seal shell victory work worthless

1. to command : to obey = captain : sailor
2. to cook : kitchen = to sleep : ________________
3. to swim : water = to fly : ________________
4. to drive : road = to walk : ________________
5. to forbid : to allow = ban : ________________
6. to lose : to win = loss : ________________
7. yes : no = to accept : to ________________
8. to sign : signature = to stamp : ________________
9. to write : to speak = written : ________________
10. treasure : valuable = garbage : ________________
11. tree : bark = egg : ________________
12. tree : leaves = book : ________________
13. shirt : sleeves = trousers : ________________
14. university : to study = factory : to ________________
15. victim : perpetrator = innocence : ________________
16. villa : to live = parking place : to ________________
17. village : city = stream : ________________
18. violin : drum = soft : ________________
19. violin : musical instrument = Italy : ________________

TEST 60

Finden Sie Wortpaare mit gegenteiliger Bedeutung.

allow answer arrive close decrease defend destroy die end go hate ~~lose~~ obey punish reap receive sell

1. to win - to lose
2. to live - to ____________
3. to love - to ____________
4. to buy - to ____________
5. to depart - to ____________
6. to forbid - to ____________
7. to attack - to ____________
8. to come - to ____________
9. to command - to ____________
10. to begin - to ____________
11. to question - to ____________
12. to build - to ____________
13. to reward - to ____________
14. to increase - to ____________
15. to send - to ____________
16. to sow - to ____________
17. to open - to ____________

TEST 61

Setzen Sie ein.

accompanied anything asleep come day example fall ~~going~~ hold kind knotty nothing notebook open other place quite swim take weather

1. ich gehe (die Treppe) hinunter > I am _going_ downstairs
2. ich weiß nichts davon > I don't know ____________ about it
3. schwimmen gehen > to go for a _______
4. sich festhalten an > to _______ fast to
5. nichts Schlimmes > ____________ serious
6. ein Beispiel geben > to give an ____________
7. ein schwieriger Punkt > a __________ problem
8. eine ganze Weile > ________ a while
9. eingeschlafen sein > to have fallen __________
10. mit anderen Worten > in ________ words
11. in Begleitung von > ___________________ by
12. in ein Heft schreiben > to write in a ______________
13. von Tag zu Tag > from _____ to day
14. krank werden > to _______ ill
15. große Augen machen > to _______ one's eyes wide
16. erstens / an erster Stelle > in the first ________
17. heute ist schönes Wetter > the _____ is fine today
18. etwas zur Kenntnis nehmen > to _______ note of
19. zu Ende gehen > to _______ to an end
20. tun Sie mir den Gefallen > be so _______ as to

TEST 62

Stimmt das?

1. Cakes are made of flour, eggs, sugar and butter. true
2. Nylon is a synthetic fibre. ________
3. Zoology is the study of plants. false
4. Like poles attract. ________
5. Canada is the largest country in North America. ________
6. The moon is bigger than the sun. ________
7. Antartica lies at the North Pole. ________
8. Coffee contains caffeine. ________
9. The capital of Australia is Melbourne. ________
10. The United States have a larger population than Canada. ______
11. Ornithology is the study of birds. ________
12. The second World War began in 1945. ________
13. Diamonds are found in mines. ________
14. The brother of my father is my brother-in-law. ________
15. The cougar is a fish. ________
16. The Sun revolves around the Earth. ________
17. French, Spanish and Romanian are romanic languages. _______
18. Oil is lighter than water. ________
19. Loch Ness is in Scotland. ________
20. Light travels faster than sound. ________

TEST 63

Setzen Sie ein.

away cannot damaged does engine glass late light nice room Should ~~serve~~ take too way weekend When Where wood your

1. Haben Sie Kinderportionen? > Do you _serve_ children's portions?
2. Wann sind Sie geboren? > _______ were you born?
3. Das Fahrzeug ist beschädigt. > The vehicle is ____________.
4. das Wochenende verbringen > to spend the ____________
5. Ich möchte ein Einzelzimmer mit Dusche. > I would like a single _______ with a shower.
6. Licht machen > to switch on the ________
7. Die Maschine verbraucht zuviel Strom. > This machine uses _____ much electricity.
8. Sie dürfen den Wagen hier nicht stehenlassen. > You __________ leave the car here.
9. Wie nett! > How _______!
10. Bitte nehmen Sie mein Gepäck. > Please ________ my luggage / baggage.
11. am späten Nachmittag > in the _______ afternoon
12. Entschuldigen Sie! / Entschuldigung! > I beg _______ pardon! / (I am) sorry!
13. Wo kann ich Briefmarken kaufen? > ________ can I buy stamps?
14. Sollen wir in den Zoo oder ins Museum gehen? > __________ we go to the zoo or the museum?
15. Holz hacken > to chop _______
16. Fort! / Verschwinde! / Raus! > Go _______!
17. Irgend etwas stimmt nicht mit dem Motor. > There is something wrong with the __________.
18. Auf welche Weise? > In what _____?
19. Nur die Ruhe! / Immer mit der Ruhe! > Easy ____ it! / Take it easy!
20. aus Glas > made of ________

TEST 64

Kreuzworträtsel

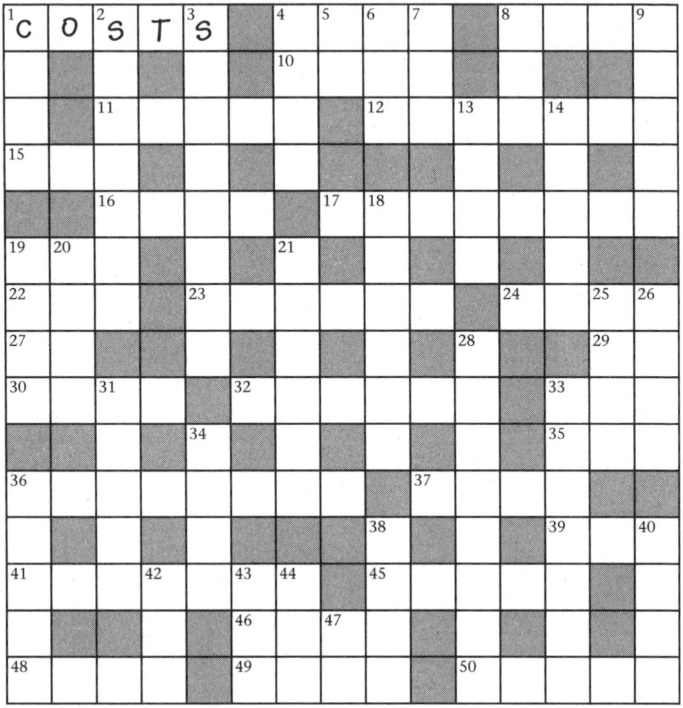

WAAGERECHT

1 The beer c**** $3.

4 T*** is a nasty remark!

8 I hate working for my b***.

10 Come h*** at once!

11 The singer has a beautiful v****.

12 I was promoted to m****** from assistant manager.

15 The blind cannot s**.

16 What's your n***?

17 You need a s******* at the beach in summer.

19 Summers in tropical countries are very h**.

22 Do you have a** cigars?

23 Use the n***** to wipe your mouth.

24 The businessmen struck a d*** after much negotiation.

27 I* is hot today!

29 S* what?

30 The bank will give you a l***.

32 I c***** swim.

33 S** down!

35 She h** three dogs.

36 He is c*******, he is always losing things.

37 Let's go i*** the house. It's getting cold.

39 R** is cheaper than whisky.

41 Wrap the food in t******, it will stay fresh.

45 The walls need a fresh coat of p****.

46 I have no t*** to meet you.

48 H*** the picture on the wall.

49 Have you s*** the movie?

50 There are 12 g**** and 15 boys in the class.

SENKRECHT

1 The c*** grazed in the pasture.

2 He is s****** years old, but in good health.

3 The children are s******* in the pool.

4 The grapes are good, buy t***.

5 H* is an excellent driver.

6 Put your a** around me. Hug me!

7 T** is cheaper than coffee.

8 She is wearing a lacy b**.

9 The tennis player has a fast s****.

13 I have a runny n***, pass me a tissue.

14 Wine is fermented g**** juice.

18 The workers have joined various trade u*****.

19 The garden was covered with h*** stones after the storm.

20 He got o*** the train.

21 He s***** fluent English.

25 Singapore is in A***.

26 The millionaire has l*** of money.

28 I hate s******* in queues.

31 The cook wears an a**** in the kitchen.

33 Though tall, she is s****** then her husband.

34 I would a*** like to see the movie.

36 Don't c**** a cold!

38 O*** the window, it is stuffy in here.

40 This room is an absolute m***. Clean it up!

42 London is sometimes blanketed by thick f**.

43 The dog wants i** food.

44 Never l** in court.

47 Can you help m*?

TEST 65

Finden Sie die logische Entsprechung.

address arrogance books button candle ~~compartment~~ Dollar East furniture gas horse length orange pointed rice snow vase week write

1. house : room = train : compartment
2. humble : arrogant = humility : ______
3. house : light = hut : ______
4. ice skates : ice = skis : ______
5. iron : metal = oxygen : ______
6. Italy : spaghetti = China : ______
7. jacket : clothing = sofa : ______
8. jacket : zipper = shirt : ______
9. January : year = Monday : ______
10. Japan : Yen = USA : ______
11. juice : bottle = flowers : ______
12. kilo : weight = meter : ______
13. kiosk : newspapers = bookstore : ______
14. knife : sharp = needle : ______
15. knife : to cut = pencil : to ______
16. lamb : sheep = foal : ______
17. left : right = West : ______
18. lemon : yellow = orange : ______
19. telephone : telephone number = letter : ______

TEST 66

Setzen Sie die Sätze in die richtige Reihenfolge.

◯ "And what does the third guy do?" the passer-by wants to know.

◯ "He puts the lanterns in the holes, but today he is ill."

◯ "There are normally three of us."

◯ A passer-by observes this happening.

◯ He asks them why they're doing that and the men explain it to him.

(1) Two men are working on a road.

◯ One of them digs a hole.

◯ The other immediately fills it up.

◯ This happens a number of times.

TEST 67

Setzen Sie ein.

another class danger deal do fun great green just latest news nice says seize ship short ~~sing~~ soap takes tap

1. falsch singen > to _sing_ out of tune
2. ich glaube es ihm > I believe what he _______
3. ich wollte gerade weggehen > I was _______ about to leave
4. sehr viel > a great _______ of
5. den Hahn zudrehen > to turn off the _____
6. sich lustig machen über > to make _____ of
7. die Gelegenheit ergreifen > to ________ the opportunity
8. die neuesten Nachrichten > the __________ news
9. ein Stück Seife > a bar of _______
10. eine Neuigkeit erfahren > to hear a piece of _______
11. einen Dienst erweisen / einen Gefallen tun > to __________ a service
12. mit dem Schiff fahren > to travel by _______
13. in Gefahr > in __________
14. in großen Mengen > in ________ quantities
15. noch ein Brot > ____________ loaf of bread
16. er sorgt für die Familie > he ________ care of the family
17. erster Klasse > first-________
18. grün anstreichen > to paint it ________
19. heute ist schönes Wetter > the weather is _______ today
20. kurz vorher > a ________ while ago

TEST 68

Setzen Sie Verwandtschaftsbezeichnungen ein.
Welches Lösungswort ergibt sich in der senkrechten Reihe?

					G	R		N	D	S		N
S		S	T		**R**							
							N	T				
					N			C				
					D			G	H	T		R
					M		T	H		R		
				S		N						
					T	W		N	S			
		N		P	**H**		W					
		N	C	L								
F		T	H		**R**							

TEST 69

Stimmt das?

1. Beethoven was a German author. false
2. The Niagara Falls are on the U.S.- Canadian border. true
3. Bees live in a hive. _________
4. A pentagon has 6 sides. _________
5. Rain comes from clouds. _________
6. Switzerland is a land-locked country. _________
7. A mile is equal to 1.6 kilometers. _________
8. Egypt is famous for pyramids. _________
9. Australia is the smallest continent in the world. _________
10. Water turns to ice at 0 degrees Celsius. _________
11. The Concorde jet is faster than the speed of sound. _________
12. Saturn is the smallest planet in our solar system. _________
13. Alexander Graham Bell invented the telephone. _________
14. Smoking causes lung disease. _________
15. Coconuts grow in cold climates. _________
16. The moon affects the tide at sea. _________
17. Greenland is the largest island in the world. _________
18. Mount Kilimanjaro is the highest mountain in the world. _____
19. One kilogram is equal to 2.2 pounds. _________
20. Steffi Graf is a Canadian tennis player. _________

TEST 70

Setzen Sie ein.

campsite complaint customs Dutch early elections ~~got~~ listen make matter meaning ninety sooner speak Spanish this thousands

1. Haben Sie einen Feuerlöscher? > Have you _got_ a fire extinguisher?
2. Radio hören > to __________ to the radio
3. Das ist eine gute Gelegenheit, Geld zu verdienen. > This is a good opportunity to __________ money.
4. Was soll das heißen? > What is the __________ of this?
5. Tausende von Menschen > __________ of people
6. über kurz oder lang / früher oder später > __________ or later
7. Ich fahre morgen sehr früh ab. > I am leaving __________ tomorrow morning.
8. Es gibt keine Demokratie ohne freie Wahlen. > There is no democracy without free __________.
9. Mein Großvater ist neunzig. > My grandfather is __________.
10. Besorg mir einen Übersetzer für Spanisch-Holländisch. > Get me an interpreter for Spanish-__________.
11. Die Sache ist erledigt! > That settles the __________!
12. Sie müssen Zoll zahlen. > You will have to pay __________ duties.
13. Wir haben Ihre Reklamation erhalten. > We confirm receipt of your __________.
14. Bitte sprechen Sie langsam. > Please __________ slowly.
15. sieh dir das an > look at __________
16. Er machte die Übersetzung vom Spanischen ins Englische. > He did a translation from __________ into English.
17. Ist hier ein Campingplatz in der Nähe? > Is there a __________ close by?

TEST 71

Setzen Sie die Buchstaben in die richtige Reihenfolge, um die gegenteilige Bedeutung zu finden.

1. export - [tmorpi] import
2. love - [eath] ____________
3. guest - [tohs] ____________
4. heat - [dolc] ____________
5. depth - [etgihh] ____________
6. length - [tarhdeb] ____________
7. life - [tehda] ____________
8. hunger - [trhtsi] ____________
9. poverty - [shirec] ____________
10. student - [eechtar] ____________
11. friend - [nmeye] ____________
12. summer - [rtinwe] ____________
13. heaven - [ellh] ____________
14. angel - [eivld] ____________
15. day - [hitgn] ____________
16. west - [tase] ____________
17. minority - [iaoyrmjt] ____________
18. lies - [trhtu] ____________
19. marriage - [cioerdv] ____________
20. happiness - [sandsse] ____________

TEST 72

Kreuzworträtsel

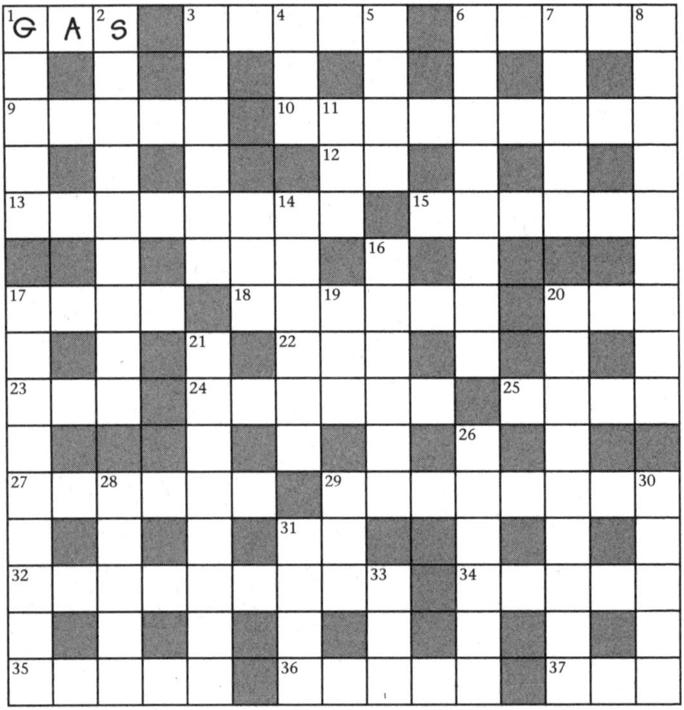

WAAGERECHT

1 We need to fill the car up with g**.

3 Dublin is an I**** city.

6 New Delhi is the capital of I****.

9 The road a**** is closed for repairs.

10 Could I borrow your pencil s********?

12 He works a* home.

13 The house is s******* on the banks of a river.

15 Delphi is in G*****.

17 The swimming p*** is dirty.

18 Meet me b***** you leave.

20 Steak and kidney p** for me, please.

22 Bring up a v** of wine from the cellar.

23 We're staying at a quiet country i**.

24 She has a very p***** face.

25 This s*** is reserved.

27 I need a can o***** to open the can.

29 I prefer l******* to orangeade.

31 Did he really say s*?

32 Take the I******** express from Frankfurt to Geneva.

34 She's d**** something important, please don't disturb her.

35 The palace is really g****, with gold carvings and antique furniture.

36 Could you e**** this data into the computer?

37 G** well soon!

SENKRECHT

1 The church has stained g**** windows.

2 The s******** soup is delicious, the corn must have been fresh.

3 Mahatma Gandhi was an I*****.

4 The dog buried i** bone in the garden.

5 The food is cold, let's h*** it up.

6 This isn't made here, it's i******* from Japan.

7 She loves to d**** at the disco.

8 They finally reached an a******** after hours of discussion.

11 He h** a fever and couldn't work.

14 I'll see you at e***** a.m.

16 Let's take him a b***** of champagne!

17 She's ill with food p********.

19 He's too f**, he has to lose weight.

20 They're p******** the house for the arrival of their guests.

21 A genie a******* out of the magic lamp.

26 We need to buy some washing p*****.

28 The additional part will cost you 24 $ e****.

29 Thanks a l** for your help.

30 She owns e**** pairs of jeans.

31 That shoe isn't available in your s***.

33 We haven't y** received your letter.

TEST 73

Setzen Sie ein.

attend break comfort extent general get glass goes loss metres minutes ~~number~~ regards shoes small speak step there train understand

1. falsch verbunden > wrong number
2. das ist kein Trost für mich > that's no ____________ to me
3. laut sprechen > to ________ in a loud voice
4. ich habe das Wort nicht verstanden > I didn't ________________ the word
5. den Zug nehmen / mit der Bahn fahren > to take a ________
6. die Schuhe anziehen > to put on one's ________
7. ein leichter Fehler > a __________ mistake
8. eine Versammlung besuchen > to __________ a meeting
9. einen Verlust erleiden > to suffer a _______
10. Sie haben 13 Stunden ohne Pause gearbeitet. > They worked 13 hours without a _______.
11. im Allgemeinen > in ____________
12. in Not geraten / in Schwierigkeiten kommen > to _____ into trouble
13. in hohem Maße > to a large __________
14. dreizehn Meter lang > thirteen __________ long
15. grüßen Sie ihn von mir > give him my ____________
16. es bleiben zwei übrig > ________ are two left
17. es ist selbstverständlich, dass > it _______ without saying that
18. auf Schritt und Tritt > at every _______ / at every turn
19. nur noch 3 Minuten > only 3 ____________ left
20. aus einem Glas trinken > to drink out of a ________

TEST 74

Finden Sie waagerecht oder senkrecht 28 Kleidungsstücke.

P	Q	C	U	N	D	E	R	S	H	I	R	T	K	W	Z
Q	B	A	D	R	E	S	S	S	W	E	A	T	E	R	B
I	E	P	Y	A	G	L	O	V	E	S	Z	J	J	H	L
W	G	C	O	S	T	U	M	E	S	A	S	D	P	N	O
S	X	W	X	B	S	O	C	K	S	S	E	E	U	Y	U
T	W	V	E	S	T	F	E	A	P	R	O	N	L	G	S
D	Q	Y	O	T	I	G	H	T	S	O	S	E	L	I	E
C	I	S	H	O	E	S	Y	F	W	O	S	G	O	G	G
B	R	A	S	S	I	E	R	E	C	V	A	D	V	Y	G
S	F	B	B	O	T	**S**	**U**	**S**	**P**	**E**	**N**	**D**	**E**	**R**	**S**
F	K	O	E	P	I	K	S	W	F	R	D	A	R	J	H
I	M	O	L	E	E	P	K	X	S	C	A	R	F	A	A
Q	O	T	T	K	Y	X	I	H	Z	O	L	S	H	C	T
N	Y	S	V	G	E	D	R	M	R	A	S	L	L	K	Q
Y	B	O	M	S	U	I	T	Y	B	T	U	I	P	E	J
A	V	G	T	R	O	U	S	E	R	S	C	P	T	T	A

TEST 75

Finden Sie die logische Entsprechung.

aquarium bald ~~bank~~ blood books Catholic daily day divorce drunk Denmark end fuel interest many match see single smoke whisper

1. letter : post office = money : bank
2. video store : videos = library : ____________
3. light : light switch = candle : ____________
4. lion : cage = fish : ____________
5. liqueur : to drink = tobacco : to ____________
6. Lisbon : Portugal = Copenhagen : ____________
7. lots : nothing = hairy : ____________
8. loud : soft = to scream : to ____________
9. love : end = marriage : ____________
10. lungs : air = heart : ____________
11. Luther : Protestant = Pope : ____________
12. magazine : newspaper = weekly : ____________
13. person : food = motor : ____________
14. marriage : children = capital : ____________
15. groom : bachelor = married : ____________
16. microphone : to speak = binoculars : to ____________
17. mineral water : sober = alcohol : ____________
18. minority : majority = few : ____________
19. moon : night = sun : ____________
20. morning : evening = beginning : ____________

TEST 76

Setzen Sie ein.

calculation call contract first fortunately fried from Hold hurry keep name number pardon put repaired school ~~speaking~~ Step successful when

1. Hallo, wer ist dort? / Wer ist am Apparat? > Who is speaking ?
2. Ich habe es eilig. > I'm in a _________.
3. Ich möchte zwei Spiegeleier. > I would like two _________ eggs.
4. Schieb die Schuld nicht auf mich! > Don't ______ the blame on me!
5. Geh zur Seite! > _______ aside!
6. sein Versprechen halten > to _______ one's promise
7. Der Elektriker hat die Sicherung repariert. > The electrician _______________ the fuse.
8. Bestellen Sie mir bitte ein Taxi. > Please get / _______ me a taxi.
9. sich unterscheiden von > to differ _______
10. Wir haben den Vertrag unterschrieben. > We signed the _______
11. Wie heißen Sie? / Wie ist Ihr Name? > What's your _______?
12. Sie sind bei rotem Licht über die Kreuzung gefahren. > You drove across the intersection _______ the lights were red.
13. Mit Ihrer Berechnung sind wir nicht einverstanden. > We are not in agreement with your ____________________.
14. Bleiben Sie am Apparat! > _______ the line!
15. ich bitte Sie um Verzeihung > I beg your ___________
16. Unterricht haben > to be at ___________
17. Können Sie mich mit dieser Nummer verbinden? > Can you connect me to this ___________?
18. vor allen Dingen > _________ of all
19. Erfolg haben > to be __________________
20. zum Glück > ____________________

TEST 77

Stimmt das?

1. An hour has three thousand six hundred seconds. true
2. A spider has 6 legs. false
3. Finnish, Hungarian and Estonian are related. _______
4. The capital of the United Kingdom is Glasgow. _______
5. My nephew is the daughter of my sister. _______
6. George Washington was the first President of the United States. _______
7. Shakespeare was an English playwright. _______
8. The capital of Switzerland is Geneva. _______
9. Tigers are found in Africa. _______
10. A football team consists of 10 players. _______
11. A tulip is a flower. _______
12. A glacier consists of ice. _______
13. The United States of America consists of 52 States. _______
14. One cannot see clearly in fog. _______
15. Kangaroos are found only in Australia. _______
16. Copper is a conductor of electricity. _______
17. Hollywood is in California. _______
18. Heavy rains cause earthquakes. _______
19. My wife's mother is my mother-in-law. _______
20. New Zealand is a part of Australia. _______

TEST 78

Setzen Sie ein.

abroad are born dig everything from gone good hard in just paper prefer reckon repaired saying stop ~~thank~~ ticket train

1. dafür danke ich Ihnen > I thank you for that
2. das sieht ihm ähnlich > that's _______ like him
3. ich habe den Zug verpasst > I've missed the _________
4. der Zug hält nicht > the train will not _______
5. fern der Heimat > far _______ home
6. die Zeitung lesen > to read the _________
7. lieber wollen > to ___________
8. ein Loch graben > to _____ a hole
9. eine Eintrittskarte lösen > to buy a ___________
10. eine schwere Arbeit > _______ work
11. Wir rechnen mit einer Lieferzeit von 8 Tagen. > We ___________ on a delivery time of 8 days.
12. alles hat seine Grenzen > there is a limit to __________________
13. im Bett liegen > to be ____ bed
14. etwas in Reparatur geben / reparieren lassen > to have something _______
15. ins Ausland reisen > to go ___________
16. er ist weg / er ist auf und davon > he has _______
17. es bleiben zwei übrig > there _____ two left
18. es ist selbstverständlich, dass > it goes without ___________ that
19. geboren werden / auf die Welt kommen > to be _______
20. gut riechen > to smell _______

Kreuzworträtsel

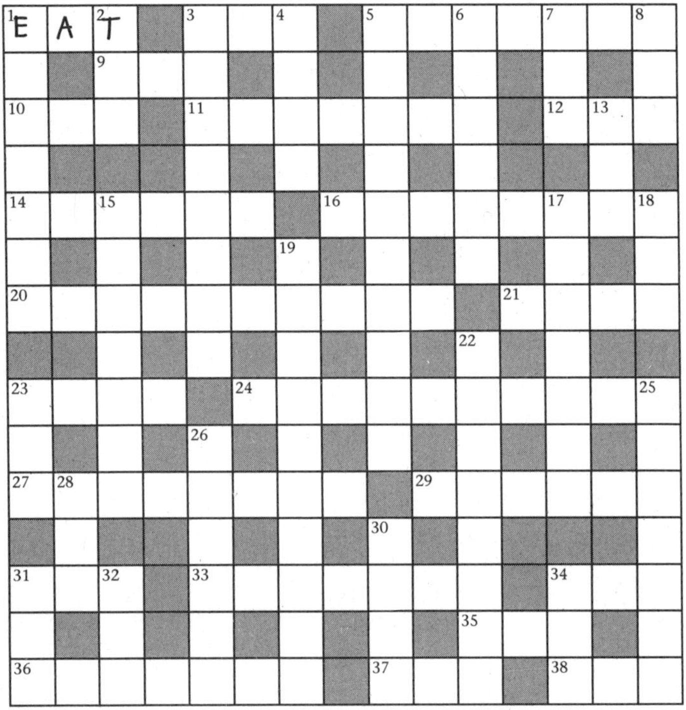

WAAGERECHT

1 I'd like to e** a pizza today.
3 Could I have a glass of t** water, please.
5 He's wearing a gold e****** in his ear.
9 He called a little while a**.
10 I'd like a boiled e** for breakfast.
11 Could I have a blue pen i****** of the red pen?
12 Please s** down.
14 The thieves r***** the house.
16 Her nylon s******* has a ladder / run (am.) in it.
20 My watch is w*********, I can swim with it.
21 He's an e*** man, he likes to see people suffer.
23 The captain and his c*** were all safe.

24 I got an i********* to the party tomorrow.

27 He used his p******* to slice the cheese.

29 The bunkers are the s***** place during war.

31 They placed a b** on the horse races.

33 Go to an ear specialist for your e****** before the pain increases.

34 That costs 25 dollars p** person.

35 He can't s** without his spectacles.

36 They d****** formally for dinner.

37 Why did you d** your hair blue?

38 Did you get a** my messages?

SENKRECHT

1 She plucked her e****** with tweezers.

2 Check the price t** on the product.

3 This row is for t******* items like soap, shampoo, etc.

4 Did you p*** the letter in time?

5 We sell e********* items like computers, etc.

6 We must r***** our expenses to stay competitive.

7 A bird will attack i** reflection in a mirror.

8 Could you g** me a tea, please.

13 We're staying at an old i**.

15 He's available b****** 5 and 6 p.m.

17 Customers must pay their i****** immediately.

18 He uses g** to slick his hair back.

19 He has been t********* to another department.

22 The J******* are known for their politeness.

23 I like his new baseball c**.

25 This is a n****** product, it has no chemicals.

26 He never knocks before he e***** a room.

28 Look me in the e** when you speak to me!

30 I*** lemonade tastes great in the summer.

31 Today was a b** day for me, everything went wrong.

32 Do t** your shoe laces or you'll trip and fall.

34 Do you like the story of the „Princess and the p**"?.

TEST 96

Setzen Sie Begriffe aus dem Bereich der Körperpflege ein. Welches Lösungswort ergibt sich in der senkrechten Reihe?

			B	R		S	**H**					
					S			P				
				S	P		**N**	G				
				P		W	**D**		R			
L		P	S	T		C	**K**					
				T		W		L				
	S	C		S	S		**R**	S				
							C		M	B		
			M			T	**H**	W		S	H	
						M		R	R		R	
					T	W			Z		R	S
				P		R	**F**		M			

TEST 81

Finden Sie Wortpaare mit gegenteiliger Bedeutung.

1. bride - [roogm] groom
2. husband - [eifw] ____________________
3. grandfather - [ertmnarhgdo] ____________________
4. son - [rgatdheu] ____________________
5. brother - [ritess] ____________________
6. uncle - [tuan] ____________________
7. nephew - [ciene] ____________________
8. widower - [iowwd] ____________________
9. gentleman - [yadl] ____________________
10. grandson - [eudnrhdgaragt] ____________________
11. morning - [vnngiee] ____________________
12. war - [ceepa] ____________________
13. old age - [otyhu] ____________________
14. departure - [iarvarl] ____________________
15. patient - [rotodc] ____________________
16. entrance - [txie] ____________________

TEST 82

Setzen Sie ein.

after arm bottom capacity cheques day duty from great injured insured lend list ~~lot~~ mail park rather shipment truth vicinity

1. viel Lärm machen > to make a lot of noise
2. Ich kann meinen rechten Arm nicht bewegen. > I cannot move my right ______.
3. Nehmen Sie Schecks an? > Do you take ______________?
4. seine Pflicht verletzen > to fail in one's ________
5. Seine intellektuellen Fähigkeiten sind toll. > His intellectual ___________ is great.
6. Der Laden ist ganztägig geöffnet. > The shop is open all ______ long.
7. Kannst du mir deinen Stift leihen? > Can you _____ me your pen?
8. offen gestanden > to tell the __________
9. Ihre Sendung habe ich erhalten. > Your ____________ has arrived.
10. Gibt es ein Einkaufszentrum in der näheren Umgebung? > Is there a shopping centre in the _______________?
11. sicher vor / geschützt gegen > safe ________
12. Hier in der Nähe gibt es einen bewachten Parkplatz. > There is a supervised car-________ near here.
13. Dieser Mann ist verletzt. > This man is ______________.
14. Sind Sie haftpflichtversichert? > Are you __________ for third party risks?
15. mit großer Mühe > with __________ difficulty
16. unten auf der Seite > at the ____________ of the page
17. vor / während / nach den Mahlzeiten > before / during / __________ meals
18. Bringen Sie mir die Weinkarte. > Can I have the wine ________, please.
19. Es ist ziemlich riskant. > It is _________ risky.
20. zur Post bringen / aufgeben > to ________ / to post

TEST 83

Finden Sie die logische Entsprechung.

aunt Asia China Europe nest nutcracker painter painting poet quiet read sometimes son ~~sunset~~ sweet team vegetable young

1. morning : evening = sunrise : sunset
2. Moscow : Russia = Beijing : ____________________
3. mother : daughter = father : ____________________
4. mouse : hole = bird : ____________________
5. Mozart : music = Picasso : ____________________
6. music : composer = poem : ____________________
7. musician : orchestra = footballer : ____________________
8. sing : paint = singer : ____________________
9. mustard : hot = sugar : ____________________
10. nephew : niece = uncle : ____________________
11. never : seldom = always : ____________________
12. music : to listen to = newspaper : to ____________________
13. Nigeria : Africa = Vietnam : ____________________
14. Nile : Africa = Rhine : ____________________
15. noise : silence = loud : ____________________
16. can : can opener = nut : ____________________
17. old man : old = baby : ____________________
18. orange : fruit = cucumber : ____________________

TEST 84

Kreuzworträtsel

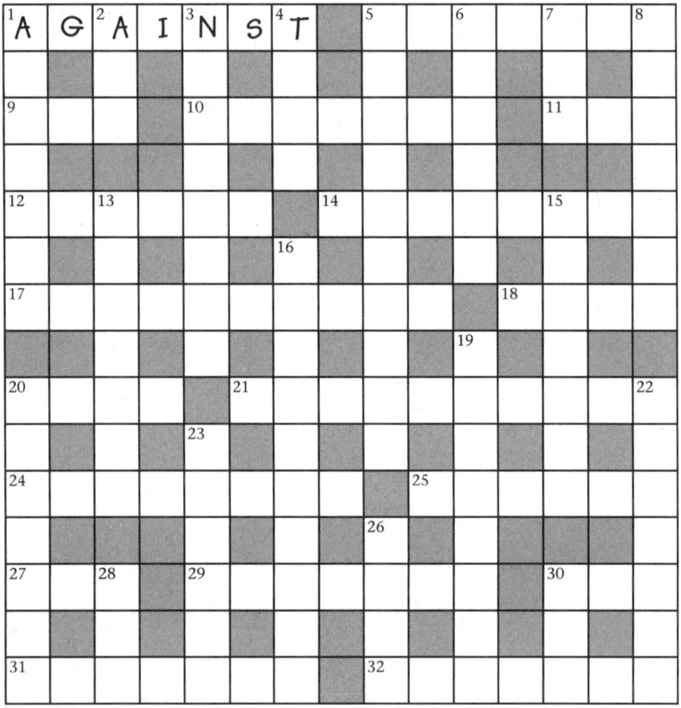

WAAGERECHT

1 I have nothing a****** him.

5 Please give us an i****** reply.

9 They have t** children, a boy and a girl.

10 C****** used to be a part of Yugoslavia.

11 That's a l**! I never took the money.

12 This c***** was built by a king in the 15th century.

14 Please sign this d*******.

17 One can pay by E********* in Europe.

18 A democracy must have a f*** press.

20 These roses are p***, not red.

21 He watches the soap opera on t********* .

24 I'd like an o******* with 2 eggs.

25 The children have l***** the alphabet.

27 Let's e**, I'm hungry.

29 Beijing is a C****** city.

30 The two countries are always at w** with each other.

31 His face is s****** due to mumps.

32 The sandwiches are packed in t****** so they won't spoil.

SENKRECHT

1 Did you read the a****** about cancer in the newspaper?

2 We lived there many years a**.

3 She's wearing a diamond n*******.

4 What t*** you so long?

5 He i********* her to me.

6 Have you visited the S***** of Liberty ?

7 A** of us are going to the party.

8 There's an interesting play at the t****** this week.

13 Isn't his behaviour s****** and unusual?

15 I called e****** this evening, but you weren't home.

16 This is a p********* zone, no vehicles are allowed.

19 She's n******* years old, next year she'll be twenty.

20 The computer can p****** a lot of data.

22 This juice has no preservatives, it is n******.

23 Please sharpen my p***** for me.

26 How much r*** do you pay for your flat?

28 He's t** lazy to do any work.

30 W** is that good-looking man?

TEST 85

Setzen Sie ein.

afternoon country course fall gloves good ground hospital late left ~~miss~~ next savings step switch understand weakness well wood work

1. das Ziel verfehlen > to miss the mark
2. ich habe es nicht verstanden > I did not ________________
3. den Motor abstellen > to __________ off the engine
4. die Handschuhe anziehen > to put on one's __________
5. Wie lange halten Sie sich in diesem Land auf? > How long are you staying in this ___________?
6. dieser Anzug sitzt gut > this suit fits _______
7. Sie hat ihre ganzen Ersparnisse aufgebraucht. > She has used up all her ________.
8. eine Schwäche haben für > to have a _____________ for
9. einen Kurs besuchen / an einem Kurs teilnehmen > to attend a __________
10. fleißig arbeiten > to _______ hard
11. im Erdgeschoss > on the __________ floor
12. am späten Nachmittag > in the late _______________
13. in Stücke gehen / springen > to _______ to pieces
14. ins Krankenhaus bringen / schaffen > to take to _____________
15. Wo ist die nächste Werkstatt? > Where is the _______ repair service / garage?
16. Vorsicht, Stufe! > Mind the _______!
17. es bleiben zwei übrig > there are two _______
18. es ist spät > it's _______
19. aus Holz > made of _______
20. gut zu Fuß sein > to be a _______ walker

TEST 86

Was passt zusammen?
Bilden Sie Sprichwörter oder Redensarten.

1. Money makes	a) a thorn.
2. Never look a gift horse	b) in his own country.
3. No man is a prophet	c) in the mouth.
4. No rose without	d) makes a thief.
5. No sweet without	e) never dies.
6. Old love	f) not make a summer.
7. One does not wash	g) one's dirty linen in public.
8. One hand washes	h) sweat.
9. One swallow does	i) the other.
10. Opportunity	j) the world go round.

11. Opposites	a) and he is bound to appear.
12. Poverty is	b) attract.
13. Practice makes	c) but silence is golden.
14. Revenge is	d) catches the worm.
15. Speak of the devil,	e) far from the tree.
16. Speech is silver	f) no sin.
17. Strike while	g) perfect.
18. The apple never falls	h) sweet.
19. The bigger they are,	i) the harder they fall.
20. The early bird	j) the iron is hot.

TEST 87

Finden Sie die logische Entsprechung.

burn ~~Brazil~~ cook fish freeze fruit fun hot Hungary melody modern monk month sad see solid tablecloth war

1. Volga : Russia = Amazon : Brazil
2. walking stick : to walk = spectacles : to ____________
3. wall : wall paper = table : ____________
4. waltz : rock music : old-fashioned : ____________
5. warm : to boil = cold : to ____________
6. Warsaw : Poland = Budapest : ____________
7. washing machine : to wash = stove : to ____________
8. water : fire = to drown : to ____________
9. water : liquid = ice : ____________
10. Wednesday : day = July : ____________
11. wheat : cereal = peach : ____________
12. white : black = happy : ____________
13. wind : storm = conflict : ____________
14. wings : birds = fins : ____________
15. winter : cold = summer : ____________
16. woman : man = nun : ____________
17. word : sentence = note : ____________
18. work : serious = games : ____________

TEST 88

Setzen Sie ein.

accept cake chicken condition enough Good know learn letters luggage more ~~Make~~ old Open pace probably right sold Sorry tomorrow

1. Mach das Beste aus dieser Gelegenheit. > Make the most of this opportunity.
2. wahrscheinlich kommt er heute nicht > he will _______________ not come today
3. Tut mir leid, falsch verbunden! > _________, wrong number!
4. man kann nie wissen > you never _______
5. Danke, das genügt. > That's ___________, thank you.
6. Ich möchte ein Brötchen mit Hähnchenfleisch. > I'd like a _____________ roll.
7. rechts fahren > to drive on the _________
8. seine helle Freude haben an > to be _______ than delighted at
9. Deutsch lernen > to _________ German
10. Öffnen Sie dieses Paket. > _______ this package.
11. Er hat sein Auto verkauft. > He _______ his car.
12. Sie ist achtzehn Jahre alt. > She is eighteen years _______.
13. Ein Stück Kuchen, bitte. > I'd like a piece of _______, please.
14. Bis morgen! > See you _______________!
15. mit schnellen Schritten > at a brisk _______
16. Akzeptieren Sie eine Kreditkarte? > Do you ___________ credit cards?
17. unter einer Bedingung > on one _________________
18. Holen Sie bitte mein Gepäck ab. > Please collect my _____________.
19. Ist Post für mich da? > Are there any _____________ for me?
20. Guten Abend! > _______ evening!

Finden Sie waagerecht oder senkrecht 29 europäische Länder.

T	I	G	F	N	C	N	D	I	Q	R	G	B	F	A	L
U	R	R	R	O	Y	S	E	C	B	X	E	U	Z	L	U
R	E	E	A	R	P	W	N	E	Z	J	R	**Y**	H	B	S
K	L	E	N	W	R	I	M	L	S	Q	M	**U**	G	A	D
E	A	C	C	A	U	T	A	A	L	B	A	**G**	L	N	P
Y	N	E	E	Y	S	Z	R	N	O	U	N	**O**	U	I	O
R	D	H	A	R	G	E	K	D	V	L	Y	**S**	X	A	R
S	W	E	D	E	N	R	J	X	A	G	S	**L**	E	Q	T
P	O	L	A	N	D	L	W	H	K	A	P	**A**	M	K	U
A	U	S	T	R	I	A	K	J	I	R	A	**V**	B	B	G
C	S	L	O	V	E	N	I	A	A	I	I	**I**	O	E	A
B	O	S	N	I	A	D	B	J	Z	A	N	**A**	U	L	L
L	K	N	E	T	H	E	R	L	A	N	D	S	R	G	Z
Z	R	I	H	U	N	G	A	R	Y	L	M	P	G	I	D
C	R	O	A	T	I	A	R	O	M	A	N	I	A	U	X
R	U	S	S	I	A	F	I	N	L	A	N	D	X	M	S

TEST 90

Finden Sie Wortpaare mit gegenteiliger Bedeutung.

black boring cheap dead far fast few hard healthy high ~~lazy~~ left light long married small southern stupid thin ugly

1. hardworking - lazy
2. large / big - ____________
3. fat - ____________
4. slow - ____________
5. beautiful - ____________
6. near - ____________
7. dark - ____________
8. expensive - ____________
9. intelligent - ____________
10. white - ____________
11. soft - ____________
12. many - ____________
13. alive - ____________
14. exciting - ____________
15. low - ____________
16. northern - ____________
17. short - ____________
18. ill - ____________
19. single - ____________
20. right - ____________

TEST 91

Setzen Sie ein.

at bill breath ~~business~~ coat created cross deserved forbidden holiday How into mood pieces problem speak television there Turn well

1. das ist nicht deine Sache > that's none of your business
2. Was kostet das Buch? > ______ much is this book?
3. ebenso gut wie > as ________ as
4. ich habe ihn zu Hause angetroffen > I found him ______ home
5. der Mantel passt mir > the ________ fits me
6. die Straße überqueren / über die Straße gehen > to __________ the street
7. ein schwieriger Punkt > a knotty ______________
8. eine gerechte Strafe > a well-________________ punishment
9. Wir haben 100 Stück auf Lager. > We have 100 _________ in stock.
10. fließend sprechen > to __________ fluently
11. im Fernsehen sehen > to see on ____________________
12. in Stücke schneiden > to cut ________ pieces
13. er hat ein Meisterwerk geschaffen > he has __________ a masterpiece
14. es donnert > __________ is thunder
15. es ist verboten zu halten > it is ____________ to stop
16. Stell das Radio an! > ________ on the radio!
17. Könnten wir bitte die Rechnung haben? > Could we have the ___________, please?
18. auf Urlaub / im Urlaub > on ______________ / on vacation
19. außer Atem > out of ____________
20. guter Laune sein / guten Mutes sein / guter Stimmung sein > to be in a good ________

TEST 92

Setzen Sie die Sätze in die richtige Reihenfolge.

◯ A spark in the machine had caused an explosion which had burnt down the whole apartment.

(1) A young man in a French town claimed he was better at household chores than his wife.

◯ He had to take care of things on his own.

◯ He learnt to iron, cook, clean and wash.

◯ He remembered that his mother had told him that gasoline cleans exceptionally well.

◯ One day he wanted to get rid of a particularly problematic stain on his clothes.

◯ So she left him.

◯ So, he poured gasoline instead of washing powder into the washing machine.

◯ The stain was also gone.

◯ Then he went shopping.

◯ When he returned, his apartment had disappeared.

TEST 93

Schreiben Sie den Text mit Leerzeichen und Satzzeichen.

THELADYWHOHADTHEMAXIMUMNUMBEROFCHILDRENINGERMA
NYLIVEDABOUT500YEARSAGOHERTOMBSTONESTATESTHATS
HEGAVEBIRTHTO38BOYSAND15GIRLSATOTALOF53BABIESTHIS
ISNOTAHIGHNUMBERWHENCOMPAREDTOARUSSIANFARMER'SWIF
EWHOISSUPPOSEDTOHAVEHAD69CHILDRENALMOSTALLOFWHOMW
EREBORNASQUADRUPLETSTRIPLETSORTWINSITISNOTKNOWN
HOWMANYOFTHEMSURVIVED

TEST 94

Setzen Sie ein.

allowed an anybody anything as cheque customers Christmas damaged ~~directory~~ help much order Right seventy skin sorry tomorrow working

1. Haben Sie ein Telefonbuch? > Have you got a telephone directory?
2. Darf man Hunde mitbringen? > Are dogs ____________?
3. Ich brauche einen Dolmetscher, der mir hilft. > I need ____ interpreter to help me.
4. Ich möchte einen Reisescheck einlösen. > I'd like to cash a traveller's _________.
5. Die meisten Kunden sind ältere Leute. > Most of the _________ are elderly people.
6. Mein Wagen wurde beschädigt. > My car has been _________.
7. er ist nur Haut und Knochen > he is nothing but _______ and bones
8. Richtig! / Das stimmt! > _________! / Quite so!
9. Die Heizung funktioniert nicht. > The heating isn't _____ properly.
10. wie gewöhnlich / wie sonst > ____ usual
11. siebzig Meter hoch > _____________ metres high
12. viel weniger > _______ less
13. Bitte deinen Papa um Hilfe. > Ask your Dad for _______.
14. Am ... habe ich bei Ihnen eine Bestellung aufgegeben. > On ... I placed an _________ with you.
15. Entschuldigen Sie! / Entschuldigung! > I beg your pardon! / (I am) _________!
16. morgen ist Sonntag > _______________ is Sunday
17. irgend etwas > something / _______________
18. Fröhliche Weihnachten! > Merry _________________!
19. Ist jemand hier? > Is _____________ there?

TEST 95

Finden Sie die logische Entsprechung.

art beverage blue calculate cars chemical colour economic fish floor hate intelligence paint ~~participants~~ penguin people roof Romania speech Slovakia

1. organisation : members = conference : participants
2. Oslo : Norway = Bucharest : ____________
3. oval : shape = pink : ____________
4. parents : children = government : ____________
5. pastor : sermon = politician : ____________
6. pasture : green = water : ____________
7. peace : war = love : ____________
8. pen : to write = calculator : to ____________
9. north pole : south pole = polar bear : ____________
10. pepper : spice = mineral water : ____________
11. person : umbrella = house : ____________
12. photo : to photograph = painting : to ____________
13. Physics : physical = Chemistry : ____________
14. wallpaper : wall = carpet : ____________
15. pigeon : bird = trout : ____________
16. polite : politeness = intelligent : ____________
17. politician : politics = artist : ____________
18. politics : political = economy : ____________
19. port : ships = car park : ____________
20. Prague : Czech Republic = Bratislava : ____________

TEST 96

Finden Sie waagerecht oder senkrecht 27 Sportarten.

F	P	K	A	L	S	W	I	M	M	I	N	G	E	G	Z
O	H	O	C	K	E	Y	L	M	S	A	I	L	I	N	G
O	K	B	S	H	S	K	A	T	I	N	G	S	J	G	V
T	F	O	Y	R	I	D	I	N	G	B	Q	D	W	L	R
B	E	X	V	C	H	E	S	S	C	T	E	N	N	I	S
A	N	I	**W**	**I**	**N**	**D**	**S**	**U**	**R**	**F**	**I**	**N**	**G**	D	P
L	C	N	S	H	B	S	J	V	Z	H	D	M	C	I	V
L	I	G	H	A	A	K	W	R	Q	U	R	O	F	N	W
B	N	D	O	N	D	I	S	O	S	R	Z	S	G	G	R
O	G	V	O	D	M	I	A	W	H	D	H	N	S	C	E
W	K	P	T	B	I	N	B	I	L	L	I	A	R	D	S
L	A	O	I	A	N	G	Z	N	D	I	V	I	N	G	T
I	R	L	N	L	T	Q	Y	G	I	N	E	E	Z	N	L
N	A	O	G	L	O	J	U	D	O	G	A	D	G	W	I
G	T	F	Z	L	N	D	G	O	L	F	L	Q	D	M	N
O	E	B	C	V	O	L	L	E	Y	B	A	L	L	X	G

TEST 97

Setzen Sie ein.

banks bear breakdown can clock country discussion first has in languages night ~~nine~~ piece pretending roll store think way without

1. halb zehn > half past nine
2. darüber lässt sich streiten > that's open to ______________
3. das versteht sich von selbst > that goes ____________ saying
4. ich habe kein Interesse daran > I am not interested ______ it
5. der, die, das erste > the ________
6. Wie alt schätzt du ihn? > How old do you ________ he is?
7. die ganze Nacht > all ________
8. Sie müssen in drei Monaten wieder ausreisen. > You must leave the ____________ again in three months.
9. ein Stück Holz > a ________ of wood
10. eine Panne haben > to have a _______________
11. einen Film entwickeln > to develop a _______ of film
12. Wir können Ihnen einen Nachlass von 10% anbieten. > We _____ give you a discount of 10%.
13. alles bleibt beim Alten > nothing _____ changed
14. im Gedächtnis behalten / sich etwas merken / etwas behalten > to _______ in mind
15. Um wieviel Uhr öffnen / schließen die Banken? > What time do the ________ open / close?
16. er tut nur so > he is just _________________
17. fremde Sprachen > foreign _______________
18. Harrods ist ein bekanntes Warenhaus > Harrods is a famous department ________
19. es ist vier Uhr > it is 4 o'________
20. auf diese Art und Weise > in that _____

TEST 98

Was passt zusammen?
Bilden Sie Sprichwörter oder Redensarten.

1.	The exception	**a)**	always goes barefoot.
2.	The leopard cannot	**b)**	by its fruit.
3.	The love of money is	**c)**	change its spots.
4.	The road to hell is paved	**d)**	is human.
5.	The shoemaker's son	**e)**	is money.
6.	The sun shines	**f)**	proves the rule.
7.	The tree is known	**g)**	the root of all evil.
8.	There are two sides	**h)**	to everything.
9.	Time	**i)**	upon all alike.
10.	To err	**j)**	with good intentions.

11.	Too many cooks	**a)**	cross to bear.
12.	We all have our	**b)**	do as the Romans do.
13.	Well begun	**c)**	is half done.
14.	When in Rome,	**d)**	spoil the broth.
15.	When the cat's away	**e)**	the forest for the trees.
16.	Where there is smoke	**f)**	the mice will play.
17.	Where there's a will	**g)**	there's a way.
18.	You can't see	**h)**	there's fire.
19.	You can't have	**i)**	without breaking eggs.
20.	You can't make an omelette	**j)**	your cake and eat it.

TEST 99

Was macht man mit dem Mund?
Finden Sie waagerecht oder senkrecht 18 Verben.

s	b	d	s	g	k	b	o	j	s	c	d	l
m	l	c	n	b	z	x	y	z	p	m	o	t
i	o	v	o	g	s	v	f	k	e	i	t	h
l	w	j	r	m	i	a	n	c	a	l	l	j
e	a	t	e	w	b	d	d	u	k	c	x	g
l	**b**	**e**	**l**	**l**	**o**	**w**	c	z	s	i	n	g
y	s	d	x	t	l	a	u	g	h	u	n	v
p	p	f	o	d	s	y	y	a	w	n	v	h
h	i	d	c	o	u	g	h	s	u	c	k	l
n	t	e	k	i	s	s	c	f	j	j	b	k
g	z	v	d	r	i	n	k	n	y	u	i	x
o	y	x	s	w	h	i	s	p	e	r	t	t
k	c	h	e	w	c	x	k	y	y	E	e	f

TEST 100

Setzen Sie ein.

blocked boring brother comfortable connected directions find ~~fish~~ insurance leg look matters receipt soon tell temper took touch translation wants

1. Haben Sie gekochtes Huhn oder gekochten Fisch? > Is there any boiled chicken or boiled fish____?
2. nach allen Seiten > in all ____________
3. Das Waschbecken ist verstopft. > The wash-basin is ____________.
4. Ich habe ein Taxi vom Flughafen genommen. > I ________ a taxi from the airport.
5. Sie müssen den Unfall Ihrer Versicherungsgesellschaft melden. > You must report the accident to your __________ company.
6. schlecht aussehen > to ________ ill
7. je mehr man hat, desto mehr man will > the more one has, the more one __________
8. Geben Sie mir eine Quittung? > May I have a ____________?
9. mein jüngerer Bruder > my younger ____________
10. sich das Bein brechen > to break one's ______
11. Die Reise war sehr bequem. > The journey was very __________.
12. Bitte nicht berühren! > Do not __________!
13. Mittel und Wege finden > to ________ ways and means
14. in Verbindung stehen mit > to be ____________ with
15. so steht die Sache > that's how ____________ stand
16. Können Sie mir sagen, wo das Konsulat ist? > Can you _______ me where the consulate is?
17. Dieser Film ist langweilig. > This movie is ____________.
18. Er machte die russisch-französische Übersetzung. > He did the Russian to French ___________.
19. wütend werden > to lose one's ____________
20. Auf Wiedersehen! / Bis bald! > Good-bye!/ So long!/ See you _____!

LÖSUNGEN

TEST 1:

1. cross **2.** aloud **3.** pick **4.** work **5.** fond **6.** different **7.** application **8.** haircut **9.** special **10.** travel **11.** map **12.** at **13.** pieces **14.** German **15.** possible **16.** send **17.** only **18.** duty **19.** be **20.** result

TEST 2:

1.	flower	vase	**I.**	bicycle	bell
2.	car	boot / trunk	**II.**	theatre	stage
3.	train	ticket	**III.**	pub	beer
4.	coffee	sugar	**IV.**	circus	clown
5.	pot	lid	**V.**	jacket	leather

a)	soup	spoon	**A)**	zoo	animals
b)	fever	thermometer	**B)**	computer	printer
c)	stairs	banisters	**C)**	sky	star
d)	sausage	mustard	**D)**	disco	music
e)	snow	ski lift	**E)**	luggage	suitcase

TEST 3:

1. interesting - boring
2. tall - short
3. rich - poor
4. sad - happy
5. new - old
6. smooth - rough
7. sharp - blunt
8. clean - dirty
9. up - down
10. top - bottom
11. fresh - stale
12. late - early
13. wet - dry
14. old - young
15. full - empty
16. right - wrong
17. transparent - opaque
18. always - never
19. heavy - light
20. polite - rude

TEST 4:

1. piece **2.** money **3.** quite **4.** listening **5.** understand **6.** Keep **7.** windshield **8.** test **9.** upset **10.** town **11.** receipt **12.** taste **13.** beginning **14.** next **15.** Can **16.** Follow **17.** recommended **18.** Turn **19.** tree

TEST 5:

1. church
2. captain
3. to eat
4. river
5. to forbid
6. Bulgaria
7. south
8. earth
9. ocean
10. Arabic
11. French
12. baker
13. milk
14. death
15. future
16. continent
17. restaurant
18. dwarf
19. mouth
20. to listen

TEST 6:

black blue brown grey green orange pink purple red white yellow

TEST 7:

1. scenery **2.** anything **3.** equals **4.** headache **5.** right **6.** Sunday **7.** cracked **8.** else **9.** educated **10.** play **11.** mistake **12.** by **13.** cinema **14.** touch **15.** head **16.** speaks **17.** times **18.** yesterday **19.** fault **20.** to

TEST 8:

1.	wall	brick
2.	hand	finger
3.	racket	tennis ball
4.	lamp	bulb
5.	banana	peel

I.	Berlin	city
II.	weather	snow
III.	night	darkness
IV.	thirst	beer
V.	bottle	cork

a.	suit	tie
b.	computer	mouse
c.	football	goal
d.	book	page
e.	coffee	sugar

A.	tree	trunk
B.	television	programme
C.	bread	slice
D.	leg	foot
E.	grammar	rules

LÖSUNGEN

TEST 9:

1. hard
2. cloud
3. happy
4. apples
5. Benelux
6. service
7. spinach
8. throat
9. weather
10. street
11. tree
12. architect
13. petrol
14. Zurich
15. hill
16. visit
17. handwriting
18. Brazil
19. fork
20. computer

TEST 10:

1. accident **2.** laughing **3.** mountain **4.** do **5.** if **6.** electrician **7.** later **8.** tooth **9.** varies **10.** will **11.** accept **12.** floor **13.** what **14.** beer **15.** water **16.** as **17.** French **18.** collect **19.** enquiry **20.** dog

TEST 11:

1. A barking dog never bites.
2. A bird in the hand is worth two in the bush.
3. A friend in need is a friend indeed.
4. A liar is not believed even when he speaks the truth.
5. A single stroke won't fell an oak.
6. Actions speak louder than words.
7. All's fair in love and war.
8. All roads lead to Rome.
9. All that glitters is not gold.
10. All things must come to an end.
11. All's well that ends well.
12. An eye for an eye, a tooth for a tooth.
13. A man's home is his castle.
14. You've made your bed, now lie in it.
15. Better late than never.
16. Big fish eat little fish.
17. Brevity is the soul of wit.
18. Caution is the mother of wisdom.
19. Cold hands, warm heart.
20. Dead men tell no tales.

TEST 12:

1. spend **2.** obliged **3.** wine **4.** wake **5.** post **6.** second **7.** dishes **8.** read **9.** enter **10.** such **11.** smoke **12.** benefit **13.** receipt **14.** this **15.** down **16.** thinking **17.** only **18.** succeeded **19.** late **20.** love

TEST 13:

1 S	P	2 E	A	3 K		4 S	5 T	6 E	A	M	7 B	O	A	8 T
E		X		N		9 T	O	Y			R			H
A		10 P	H	O	N	E		11 E	A	12 R	A	13 C	H	E
14 S	E	E		C		W				E		I		I
O		15 C	A	K	E		16 S	17 T	R	A	N	G	E	R
N		T		I		18 O		A		D		A		
19 I	20 T	S		21 N	A	P	22 K	I	N		23 T	R	24 E	25 E
26 N	O			G		27 E	E	L		28 M			29 A	M
30 G	E	31 T	S		32 A	N	Y	O	N	E		33 A	R	E
		I		34 I		E		R		D		N		R
35 L	E	M	O	N	A	D	E		36 K	I	L	O		G
I		E		T				37 T		C		38 T	I	E
39 L	E	S	40 S	O	N	41 S		42 I	R	I	S	H		N
A			E			43 A	44 I	R		N		E		C
45 C	I	G	A	R	E	T	T	E		46 E	A	R	L	Y

LÖSUNGEN

TEST 14:

		R	**H**	I	N	O	C	E	R	O	S
		G	**I**	R	A	F	F	E			
			P	E	N	G	U	I	N		
E	L	E	**P**	H	A	N	T				
		F	**O**	X							
L	E	O	**P**	A	R	D					
		W	**O**	L	F						
			T	I	G	E	R				
	B	E	**A**	R							
	C	A	**M**	E	L						
		T	**U**	R	T	L	E				
			S	N	A	K	E				

TEST 15:

1. glasses **2.** racket **3.** fear **4.** Mexicans **5.** Greece **6.** Christianity **7.** rooms **8.** station **9.** expensive **10.** bell **11.** engine **12.** leg **13.** floor **14.** restaurant **15.** slow **16.** box **17.** Koran **18.** study **19.** liver **20.** healthy

TEST 16:

1. so **2.** vegetables **3.** never **4.** stay **5.** morning **6.** meat **7.** Leave **8.** people **9.** change **10.** cut **11.** fastest **12.** age **13.** Catholic **14.** running **15.** placed **16.** used **17.** finish **18.** been **19.** books **20.** only

L Ö S U N G E N

TEST 17:

1. Do not throw pearls before swine.
2. Don't count your chickens before they hatch.
3. Easy come, easy go.
4. Faith will move mountains.
5. First come, first served.
6. Fish and wine go together.
7. Four eyes see more than two.
8. God helps those who help themselves.
9. He who laughs last, laughs longest.
10. Honey catches more flies than vinegar.
11. Honour to whom honour is due.
12. If you grease well, you speed well.
13. In the country of the blind, the one-eyed man is king.
14. It is better to give than to receive.
15. Knowledge is power.
16. Lies have short legs.
17. Little thieves are hanged, but great ones escape.
18. Love is blind.
19. Lucky at cards, unlucky in love.
20. Man proposes, God disposes.

TEST 18:

1. envelope
2. breathe
3. leather
4. dry
5. Egypt
6. beggar
7. rubber
8. steal
9. drops
10. Austria
11. seats
12. bird
13. French
14. dangerous
15. rain
16. Christmas
17. baker
18. truth
19. notes
20. frame

TEST 19:

1. comfort **2.** lose **3.** trust **4.** Sit **5.** milk **6.** exchange **7.** Look **8.** fits **9.** sign **10.** pass **11.** profession **12.** electricity **13.** children **14.** name **15.** than **16.** today **17.** car **18.** table **19.** feel **20.** learn

TEST 20:

1. chin	beard
2. church	pope
3. lightning	thunder
4. wine	glass
5. car	petrol

I. tree	wood
II. face	nose
III. question	answer
IV. judge	verdict
V. cause	effect

a. shirt	collar
b. sports	Olympics
c. sky	cloud
d. music	notes
e. word	letters

A. heater	warmth
B. plant	leaf
C. money	wallet
D. apartment	rent
E. parties	elections

TEST 21:

1. fingernail **2.** shoulder **3.** stomach **4.** eyebrow **5.** tongue **6.** throat **7.** finger **8.** breast **9.** tooth **10.** thumb **11.** mouth **12.** cheek **13.** bosom **14.** beard **15.** skin **16.** nose **17.** neck **18.** knee **19.** head **20.** hand **21.** hair **22.** face **23.** chin **24.** bone

TEST 22:

1. here **2.** or **3.** turn **4.** care **5.** whenever **6.** less **7.** manners **8.** yesterday **9.** tell **10.** about **11.** were **12.** voice **13.** please **14.** radio **15.** hand **16.** morning **17.** glad **18.** about **19.** home **20.** long

TEST 23:

1. to give - to take
2. to accept - to refuse
3. to freeze - to melt
4. to push - to pull
5. to approve - to disapprove
6. to lock - to unlock
7. to succeed - to fail
8. to appear - to disappear
9. to lend - to borrow
10. to ascend - to descend
11. to search - to find
12. to trust - to distrust
13. to break - to fix
14. to halve - to double
15. to forget - to remember
16. to agree - to disagree
17. to tie - to untie
18. to behave - to misbehave
19. to throw - to catch
20. to follow - to lead

TEST 24:

										The						
						S	P	A	I	**N**						
								S	W	**E**	D	E	N			
										T	U	R	K	E	Y	
										H	U	N	G	A	R	Y
						S	L	O	V	**E**	N	I	A			
										R	U	S	S	I	A	
									S	**L**	O	V	A	K	I	A
				P	O	R	T	U	G	**A**	L					
						R	O	M	A	**N**	I	A				
S	W	I	T	Z	E	R	L	A	N	**D**						
						Y	U	G	O	**S**	L	A	V	I	A	

TEST 25:

1. plastic **2.** cook **3.** stroke **4.** matter **5.** thing **6.** glasses **7.** hands **8.** run **9.** Summer **10.** history **11.** slow **12.** temperature **13.** taste **14.** day **15.** Where **16.** raining **17.** razor **18.** May **19.** case **20.** sharp

TEST 26:

1. stage
2. conductor
3. dead
4. temperature
5. uniform
6. to roar
7. white
8. glass
9. heater
10. to write
11. referee
12. police
13. red
14. cutlery
15. glass
16. hard
17. person
18. peace
19. darkness
20. Indonesia

TEST 27:

1 P	A	2 I	N	3 T	E	4 D		5 D		6 T	R	7 I	E	D
R		N		U		I		E		R		R		
8 O	F	F	E	R		9 F	A	C	T	O	R	I	E	10 S
U		L		K		F		K		U		S		W
11 D	I	A	B	E	T	I	C		12 A	S	T	H	M	A
		T		Y		C		13 A		E				L
14 S	H	I	P		15 S	U	16 P	P	E	R		17 A	L	L
E		O		18 R		19 L	I	P		S		E		O
20 V	A	N		21 E	N	T	E	R	S		22 B	R	E	W
E				M		Y		O		23 A		O		
24 N	E	25 P	H	E	W		26 B	A	G	P	I	P	E	27 S
T		R		M		28 M		C		P		L		W
29 H	A	I	R	B	R	U	S	H		30 L	E	A	V	E
		N		E		C		E		E		N		E
31 E	N	T	E	R		H		32 D	E	S	S	E	R	T

TEST 28:

1. reason **2.** enough **3.** would **4.** drive **5.** younger **6.** do **7.** with **8.** health **9.** well **10.** times **11.** quarter **12.** walk **13.** hardly **14.** turn **15.** rule **16.** touch **17.** tomorrow **18.** not **19.** there **20.** better

TEST 29:

1. autumn / fall (am.) **2.** July **3.** seven **4.** Thursday **5.** stars **6.** February **7.** four **8.** backward **9.** Wednesday **10.** third **11.** today **12.** never **13.** South **14.** future **15.** above

TEST 30:

1 C	U	2 P		3 B	R	4 I	E	5 F		6 A	7 C	T	8 O	R
A		O		R		N		L			A		U	
9 R	H	I	N	E		10 T	R	A	N	11 S	P	12 O	R	T
		S		A		R		T		H		W		
13 B	O	O	K	S	H	O	P		14 P	R	I	E	S	15 T
		N		T		D		16 C		I				H
17 S	U	I	T		18 M	U	19 S	E	U	M		20 A	G	E
L		N		21 O		22 C	A	N		P		M		R
23 E	G	G		24 P	R	E	T	T	Y		25 A	B	L	E
E				E		D		I		26 B		U		
27 P	O	28 L	A	N	D		29 U	M	B	R	E	L	L	A
		I		E		30 H		E		A		A		
31 I	32 M	P	33 O	R	T	A	N	T		34 N	I	N	T	35 H
	E		F			V		R		D		C		E
36 K	N	I	F	E		37 E	V	E	R	Y		38 E	A	R

TEST 31:
1. salt **2.** Make **3.** coming **4.** damage **5.** performance **6.** drink **7.** car **8.** machine **9.** hospital **10.** charge **11.** No **12.** sea **13.** Noon **14.** shoes **15.** Good **16.** door **17.** dog **18.** God **19.** surprise **20.** too

TEST 32:

1. crocodile
2. day
3. fleet
4. head
5. twelve
6. shampoo
7. deep
8. to hiss
9. summer
10. to lie
11. boss
12. water
13. verse
14. fork
15. oil
16. Dutch
17. beautiful
18. to drink
19. to reap
20. round

TEST 33:

A man has a sausage stand directly opposite a bank. An old friend comes and asks him: „Can you lend me some money?". „I'm sorry, I can't!" - „And why not?" - „Because I have a contract with the bank!" - „What kind of a contract?" - „I don't lend any money and they don't sell any sausages!"

TEST 34:

1. south **2.** nowhere **3.** back **4.** going **5.** watch **6.** something **7.** coat **8.** cross **9.** people **10.** bread **11.** question **12.** carry **13.** same **14.** advance **15.** fact **16.** age **17.** until **18.** need **19.** something **20.** mistake

TEST 35:

1. Danish
2. water
3. plant
4. mew
5. to swim
6. dinner
7. small
8. nose
9. salary
10. republic
11. season
12. architecture
13. deaf
14. to hear
15. cold
16. nearness
17. thin
18. princess

TEST 36:

1. direct - indirect
2. perfect - imperfect
3. loose - tight
4. together - separate
5. yesterday - tomorrow
6. flexible - inflexible
7. liquid - solid
8. now - later
9. offensive - defensive
10. noisy - quiet
11. scarce - abundant
12. arid - fertile
13. tolerant - intolerant
14. spicy - bland
15. arrogant - humble
16. plausible - implausible
17. shortsighted - longsighted
18. strong - weak

TEST 37:

1. any **2.** great **3.** Take **4.** would **5.** Welcome **6.** park **7.** another **8.** That **9.** skidded **10.** meet **11.** seriously **12.** over **13.** parking **14.** page **15.** ago **16.** nationality **17.** back **18.** road **19.** coffee **20.** hundreds

L Ö S U N G E N

TEST 38:

1. arms
2. teeth
3. brain
4. lips
5. fist
6. nose
7. eyes
8. ears
9. tongue
10. heart
11. hands
12. finger
13. skin
14. hair
15. beard
16. neck
17. lungs
18. muscles
19. foot
20. legs

TEST 39:

[1]B	[2]A	[3]R		[4]S	P	[5]O	R	[6]T		[7]C	H	[8]E	A	[9]P
[10]A	G	E		A		U		E		U		X		R
[11]L	O	C	A	L		[12]T	R	A	N	S	L	A	T	E
L		E		A				M		T		C		V
[13]S	E	P	A	R	A	[14]T	E		[15]B	O	T	T	L	E
		T		Y		O		[16]N		M				N
[17]A	S	I	A		[18]A	N	[19]Y	O	N	E		[20]V	A	T
S		O		[21]A		[22]G	E	T		R		A		E
[23]P	E	N		[24]C	O	U	S	I	N		[25]I	C	E	D
A				C		E		C		[26]D		C		
[27]R	E	[28]P	A	I	R		[29]C	E	R	A	M	I	C	[30]S
A		R		D		[31]F				N		N		P
[32]G	U	I	D	E	B	O	O	[33]K		[34]G	R	A	[35]P	E
U		Z		N		O		E		E		[36]T	I	E
[37]S	W	E	E	T		[38]D	R	Y	E	R		[39]E	N	D

TEST 40:

1. bad **2.** hungry **3.** ought **4.** weather **5.** aches **6.** understand **7.** rising **8.** rate **9.** funny **10.** pay **11.** coat **12.** Our **13.** height **14.** else **15.** on **16.** thirteen **17.** tomorrow **18.** nothing **19.** else **20.** side

LÖSUNGEN

TEST 41:

1 Who **2** Where **3** Where **4** What **5** Who **6** Whom **7** How **8** Whose **9** Which **10** How **11** How **12** How **13** When **14** Why **15** Where **16** What **17** What **18** What **19** Since **20** Till

TEST 42:

1. sand
2. Greece
3. match
4. to stand
5. sky
6. fish
7. dolphin
8. Bavarian
9. December
10. goat
11. pencil
12. Europe
13. pot
14. friendly
15. spider
16. tomatoes
17. book
18. face
19. strong
20. hat

TEST 43:

1. declare **2.** latest **3.** give **4.** car **5.** night **6.** outdoors **7.** faithful **8.** television **9.** judge **10.** worry **11.** excludes **12.** other **13.** sick **14.** corner **15.** no **16.** by **17.** try **18.** need **19.** sauna **20.** present

TEST 44:

1. mayor
2. Spain
3. head
4. to sing
5. familiar
6. visitors
7. sweet
8. to believe
9. dry
10. Scandinavia
11. rocket
12. university
13. patient
14. to close
15. lazy
16. dog
17. divide
18. departure
19. defence
20. to finish

TEST 45:

1. stone
2. necklace
3. effect
4. barn
5. lungs
6. gun
7. to shoot
8. chocolate
9. animal
10. finger
11. licence
12. vodka
13. to slither
14. ashtray
15. kitchen
16. poor
17. city
18. brother
19. to explode
20. cheap

TEST 46:

1. trusted **2.** parking **3.** tune **4.** What **5.** doctor **6.** third **7.** Germany **8.** passed **9.** beautiful **10.** song **11.** task **12.** hour **13.** early **14.** garage **15.** Speak **16.** masterpiece **17.** in **18.** there **19.** stomach **20.** bicycle

TEST 47:

active
athletic
attractive
balanced
beautiful
brave
charming
cheerful
clean
elegant
exciting
fair
friendly
generous
hardworking
helpful
honest
humorous
intelligent
jolly
loving
neat
nice
optimistic
patient
polite
pretty
punctual
quiet
reliable
responsible
rich
sociable
strong
sympathetic
thin
tolerant
versatile

TEST 48:

1 M		2 Y	E	3 S		4 O	P	5 E	R	6 A		7 S	O	8 N
O		E		9 C	A	R		X		G		H		I
10 P	A	S	T	A		11 C	H	A	I	R		12 I	C	E
E		T		L		H		C		E		F		C
13 D	Y	E		14 E	Y	E		15 T	16 H	E	A	T	17 R	E
		R				S			18 A	M			U	
19 I	N	D	I	20 A		21 T	H	22 E	S	E		23 A	N	24 D
T		A		U		R		X		N		E		I
25 S	26 A	Y		27 S	28 T	A	M	P		29 T	I	R	E	D
	G			30 T	O			L				O		
31 C	O	32 N	T	R	O	33 L		34 A	R	35 E		36 P	E	37 A
O		U		A		E		I		X		L		N
38 A	I	R		39 L	E	A	R	N		40 T	R	A	I	N
S		S		I		V		41 E	A	R		N		O
42 T	H	E		43 A	H	E	A	D		44 A	G	E		Y

TEST 49:

1. forward **2.** remember **3.** would **4.** if **5.** change **6.** advice **7.** little **8.** broken **9.** break **10.** light **11.** less **12.** This **13.** thanks **14.** Good **15.** make **16.** your **17.** school **18.** soon **19.** some **20.** reserve

TEST 50:

1. vertical - horizontal
2. boisterous - calm
3. feminine - masculine
4. pessimistic - optimistic
5. microscopic - gigantic
6. famous - unknown
7. generous - stingy
8. colorful - drab
9. wild - tame
10. bare - covered
11. legal - illegal
12. temporary - permanent
13. physical - spiritual

TEST 51:

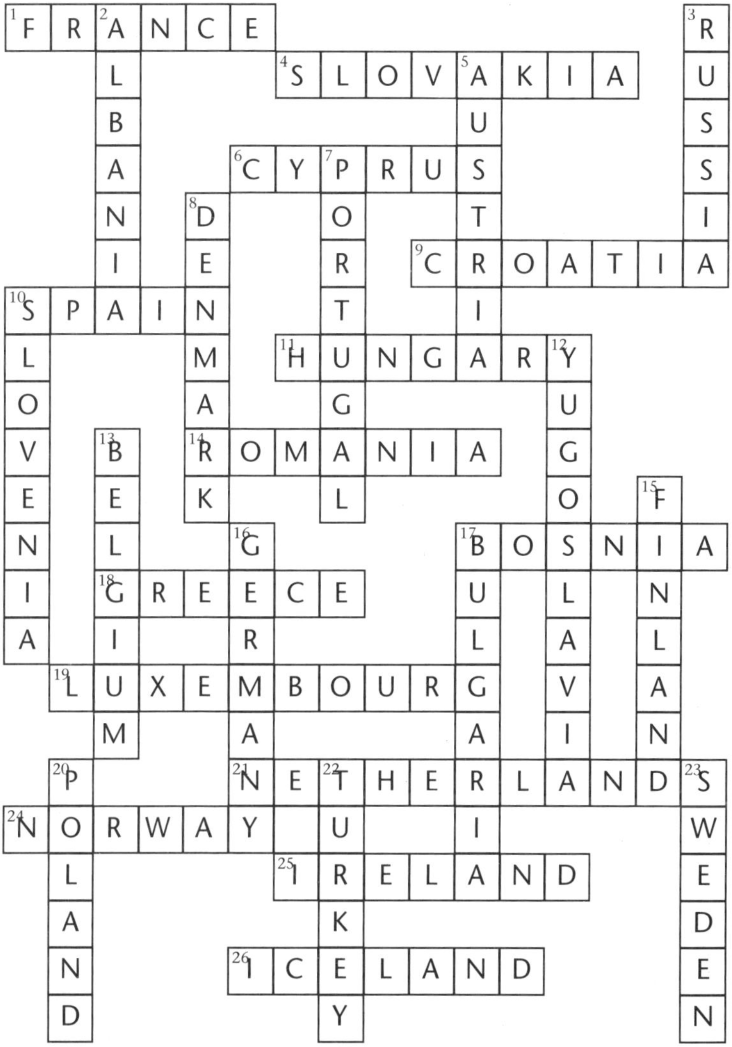

TEST 52:

1. cards **2.** enough **3.** want **4.** Have **5.** contact **6.** eggs **7.** left **8.** quarrel **9.** spoilt **10.** country **11.** once **12.** matches **13.** look **14.** beach **15.** outside **16.** out **17.** Shut **18.** repair **19.** doctor **20.** lose

LÖSUNGEN

TEST 53:

1. Peter goes to a fortune teller to ask about his future.
2. She looks into a crystal ball for a long time and then tells him:
3. "You will be very rich if you do exactly as I tell you."
4. "Wait for a clear night with a full moon and go to the old graveyard at midnight."
5. "Take a spade with you and dig for treasure."
6. "You'll find the treasure a few metres under the ground."
7. "Beware! If you think of noodle soup while you are digging, you won't find it."
8. Peter is excited about the treasure and buys himself a spade.
9. On a clear night with a full moon he goes to the graveyard and begins to dig.
10. Suddenly he throws down the spade and runs away:
11. "Damn! I've never thought of noodle soup in my life!"
12. „But now I can't get it out of my head!"

TEST 54:

1. disadvantage
2. failure
3. desert
4. sour
5. stop
6. alone
7. to blow
8. arrow
9. screw
10. shoe
11. to kiss
12. to cry
13. emotions
14. to see
15. devil
16. Ireland
17. stewardess
18. unemployed

TEST 55:

1. May **2.** cold **3.** same **4.** black **5.** two **6.** teeth **7.** faintest **8.** welcome **9.** soul **10.** these **11.** worse **12.** right **13.** fault **14.** of **15.** from **16.** else **17.** best **18.** first **19.** banks **20.** for

TEST 56:

1. false
2. true
3. true
4. true
5. true
6. false
7. true
8. true
9. true
10. true
11. false
12. false
13. true
14. false
15. true
16. false
17. true
18. false
19. true
20. false

TEST 57:

[1]M	U	[2]S	I	[3]C		[4]R	E	[5]D		[6]A	P	[7]P	L	[8]E
E		O		[9]I	C	E		A		I		H		N
[10]A	R	M		N		[11]M	O	T	O	R		[12]O	L	D
N		E		E		A		E		P		T		
[13]S	[14]A	W		[15]M	O	R	E		[16]A	L	M	O	N	[17]D
	[18]T	H		A		K		[19]T		A				A
[20]H	E	E	L		[21]W	A	S	H	I	N	G	[22]T	O	N
A		R		[23]E		B		R		E		R		C
[24]T	H	E	M	S	E	L	V	E	S		[25]R	A	[26]T	E
E				C		Y		A		[27]T		[28]N	O	
[29]S	A	[30]N	D	A	L		[31]S	T	A	R		[32]S	E	[33]T
		E		L		[34]W		E		A		P		H
[35]H	E	R		[36]O	N	I	O	N		V		[37]O	N	E
O		V		P		N		[38]E	Y	E		R		R
[39]W	H	E	R	E		[40]D	I	D		[41]L	I	T	R	E

TEST 58:

1. by **2.** lot **3.** vanilla **4.** pace **5.** holds **6.** shop **7.** recommended **8.** battery **9.** took **10.** his **11.** understands **12.** Open **13.** sample **14.** party **15.** taste **16.** limit **17.** luck **18.** or **19.** Cheer **20.** minute

LÖSUNGEN

TEST 59:

1. sailor
2. bedroom
3. air
4. pavement
5. permission
6. victory
7. to refuse
8. seal
9. oral
10. worthless
11. shell
12. pages
13. legs
14. work
15. guilt
16. to park
17. river
18. loud
19. country

TEST 60:

1. to win - to lose
2. to live - to die
3. to love - to hate
4. to buy - to sell
5. to depart - to arrive
6. to forbid - to allow
7. to attack - to defend
8. to come - to go
9. to command - to obey
10. to begin - to end
11. to question - to answer
12. to build - to destroy
13. to reward - to punish
14. to increase - to decrease
15. to send - to receive
16. to sow - to reap
17. to open - to close

TEST 61:

1. going **2.** anything **3.** swim **4.** hold **5.** nothing **6.** example **7.** knotty **8.** quite **9.** asleep **10.** other **11.** accompanied **12.** notebook **13.** day **14.** fall **15.** open **16.** place **17.** weather **18.** take **19.** come **20.** kind

TEST 62:

1. true
2. true
3. false
4. false
5. true
6. false
7. false
8. true
9. false
10. true
11. true
12. false
13. true
14. false
15. false
16. false
17. true
18. true
19. true
20. true

L Ö S U N G E N

TEST 63:

1. serve **2.** When **3.** damaged **4.** weekend **5.** room **6.** light **7.** too **8.** cannot **9.** nice **10.** take **11.** late **12.** your **13.** Where **14.** Should **15.** wood **16.** away **17.** engine **18.** way **19.** does **20.** glass

TEST 64:

[1]C	O	[2]S	T	[3]S		[4]T	[5]H	[6]A	[7]T		[8]B	O	S	[9]S
O		E		W		[10]H	E	R	E		R			E
W		[11]V	O	I	C	E		[12]M	A	[13]N	A	[14]G	E	R
[15]S	E	E		M		M				O		R		V
		[16]N	A	M	E		[17]S	[18]U	N	S	H	A	D	E
[19]H	[20]O	T		I		[21]S		N		E		P		
[22]A	N	Y		[23]N	A	P	K	I	N		[24]D	E	[25]A	[26]L
[27]I	T			G		E		O		[28]S			[29]S	O
[30]L	O	[31]A	N		[32]C	A	N	N	O	T		[33]S	I	T
		P		[34]A		K		S		A		[35]H	A	S
[36]C	A	R	E	L	E	S	S		[37]I	N	T	O		
A		O		S				[38]O		D		[39]R	U	[40]M
[41]T	I	N	[42]F	O	[43]I	[44]L		[45]P	A	I	N	T		E
C			O		[46]T	I	[47]M	E		N		E		S
[48]H	A	N	G		[49]S	E	E	N		[50]G	I	R	L	S

TEST 65:

1. compartment
2. arrogance
3. candle
4. snow
5. gas
6. rice
7. furniture
8. button
9. week
10. Dollar
11. vase
12. length
13. books
14. pointed
15. to write
16. horse
17. East
18. orange
19. address

LÖSUNGEN

TEST 66:

1. Two men are working on a road.
2. One of them digs a hole.
3. The other immediately fills it up.
4. This happens a number of times.
5. A passer-by observes this happening.
6. He asks them why they're doing that and the men explain it to him.
7. "There are normally three of us."
8. "And what does the third guy do?" the passer-by wants to know.
9. "He puts the lanterns in the holes, but today he is ill."

TEST 67:

1. sing **2.** says **3.** just **4.** deal **5.** tap **6.** fun **7.** seize **8.** latest
9. soap **10.** news **11.** do **12.** ship **13.** danger **14.** great
15. another **16.** takes **17.** class **18.** green **19.** nice **20.** short

TEST 68:

					G	R	A	N	D	S	O	N
S	I	S	T	E	**R**							
					A	U	N	T				
					N	I	E	C	E			
					D	A	U	G	H	T	E	R
					M	O	T	H	E	R		
				S	**O**	N						
					T	W	I	N	S			
		N	E	P	**H**	E	W					
	U	N	C	L	**E**							
F	A	T	H	E	**R**							

TEST 69:

1. false
2. true
3. true
4. false
5. true
6. true
7. true
8. true
9. true
10. true
11. true
12. false
13. true
14. true
15. false
16. true
17. true
18. false
19. true
20. false

TEST 70:

1. got **2.** listen **3.** make **4.** meaning **5.** thousands **6.** sooner **7.** early **8.** elections **9.** ninety **10.** Dutch **11.** matter **12.** customs **13.** complaint **14.** speak **15.** this **16.** Spanish **17.** site

TEST 71:

1. export - import
2. love - hate
3. guest - host
4. heat - cold
5. depth - height
6. length - breadth
7. life - death
8. hunger - thirst
9. poverty - riches
10. student - teacher
11. friend - enemy
12. summer - winter
13. heaven - hell
14. angel - devil
15. day - night
16. west - east
17. minority - majority
18. lies - truth
19. marriage - divorce
20. happiness - sadness

LÖSUNGEN

TEST 72:

[1]G	A	[2]S		[3]I	R	[4]I	S	[5]H		[6]I	N	[7]D	I	[8]A
L		W		N		T		E		M		A		G
[9]A	H	E	A	D		[10]S	[11]H	A	R	P	E	N	E	R
S		E		I			[12]A	T		O		C		E
[13]S	I	T	U	A	T	[14]E	D		[15]G	R	E	E	C	E
		C		N		L		[16]B		T				M
[17]P	O	O	L		[18]B	E	[19]F	O	R	E		[20]P	I	E
O		R		[21]A		[22]V	A	T		D		R		N
[23]I	N	N		[24]P	R	E	T	T	Y		[25]S	E	A	T
S				P		N		L		[26]P		P		
[27]O	P	[28]E	N	E	R		[29]L	E	M	O	N	A	D	[30]E
N		X		A		[31]S	O			W		R		I
[32]I	N	T	E	R	C	I	T	[33]Y		[34]D	O	I	N	G
N		R		E		Z		E		E		N		H
[35]G	R	A	N	D		[36]E	N	T	E	R		[37]G	E	T

TEST 73:

1. number **2.** comfort **3.** speak **4.** understand **5.** train **6.** shoes **7.** small **8.** attend **9.** loss **10.** break **11.** general **12.** get **13.** extent **14.** metres **15.** regards **16.** there **17.** goes **18.** step **19.** minutes **20.** glass

TEST 74:

1. UNDERSHIRT **2.** SUSPENDERS **3.** TIGHTS **4.** BRA(SSIERE) **5.** PULLOVER **6.** OVERCOAT **7.** TROUSERS **8.** SANDALS **9.** COSTUME **10.** SWEATER **11.** JACKET **12.** GLOVES **13.** BLOUSE **14.** BOOTS **15.** SOCKS **16.** APRON **17.** SHOES **18.** DRESS **19.** SCARF **20.** SKIRT **21.** VEST **22.** SHIRT **23.** SLIP **24.** BELT **25.** SUIT **26.** CAP **27.** TIE **28.** HAT

TEST 75:

1. bank
2. books
3. match
4. aquarium
5. to smoke
6. Denmark
7. bald
8. to whisper
9. divorce
10. blood
11. Catholic
12. daily
13. fuel
14. interest
15. single
16. to see
17. drunk
18. many
19. day
20. end

TEST 76:

1. speaking **2.** hurry **3.** fried **4.** put **5.** Step **6.** keep **7.** repaired **8.** call **9.** from **10.** contract **11.** name **12.** when **13.** calculation **14.** Hold **15.** pardon **16.** school **17.** number **18.** first **19.** successful **20.** fortunately

TEST 77:

1. true
2. false
3. true
4. false
5. false
6. true
7. true
8. false
9. false
10. false
11. true
12. true
13. false
14. true
15. true
16. true
17. true
18. false
19. true
20. false

TEST 78:

1. thank **2.** just **3.** train **4.** stop **5.** from **6.** paper **7.** prefer **8.** dig **9.** ticket **10.** hard **11.** reckon **12.** everything **13.** in **14.** repaired **15.** abroad **16.** gone **17.** are **18.** saying **19.** born **20.** good

TEST 79:

1 E	A	2 T		3 T	A	4 P		5 E	A	6 R	R	7 I	N	8 G
Y		9 A	G	O		O		L		E		T		E
10 E	G	G		11 I	N	S	T	E	A	D		12 S	13 I	T
B				L		T		C		U			N	
14 R	O	15 B	B	E	D		16 S	T	O	C	K	17 I	N	18 G
O		E		T		19 T		R		E		N		E
20 W	A	T	E	R	P	R	O	O	F		21 E	V	I	L
		W		Y		A		N		22 J		O		
23 C	R	E	W		24 I	N	V	I	T	A	T	I	O	25 N
A		E		26 E		S		C		P		C		A
27 P	28 E	N	K	N	I	F	E		29 S	A	F	E	S	T
	Y			T		E		30 I		N				U
31 B	E	32 T		33 E	A	R	A	C	H	E		34 P	E	R
A		I		R		E		E		35 S	E	E		A
36 D	R	E	S	S	E	D		37 D	Y	E		38 A	L	L

TEST 80:

BRUS**H**
SO**A**P
SPO**N**GE
POW**D**ER
LIPSTIC**K**
TOW**E**L
SCISSO**R**S
COMB
MOUT**H**WASH
M**I**RROR
TW**E**EZERS
PER**F**UME

TEST 81:

1. bride - groom
2. husband - wife
3. grandfather - grandmother
4. son - daughter
5. brother - sister
6. uncle - aunt
7. nephew - niece
8. widower - widow
9. gentleman - lady
10. grandson - granddaughter
11. morning - evening
12. war - peace
13. old age - youth
14. departure - arrival
15. patient - doctor
16. entrance - exit

TEST 82:

1. lot **2.** arm **3.** cheques **4.** duty **5.** capacity **6.** day **7.** lend **8.** truth **9.** shipment **10.** vicinity **11.** from **12.** park **13.** injured **14.** insured **15.** great **16.** bottom **17.** after **18.** list **19.** rather **20.** mail

TEST 83:

1. sunset
2. China
3. son
4. nest
5. painting
6. poet
7. team
8. painter
9. sweet
10. aunt
11. sometimes
12. read
13. Asia
14. Europe
15. quiet
16. nutcracker
17. young
18. vegetable

LÖSUNGEN

TEST 84:

1 A	G	2 A	I	3 N	S	4 T		5 I	N	6 S	T	7 A	N	8 T
R		G		E		O		N		T		L		H
9 T	W	O		10 C	R	O	A	T	I	A		11 L	I	E
I				K		K		R		T				A
12 C	A	13 S	T	L	E		14 D	O	C	U	M	15 E	N	T
L		T		A		16 P		D		E		A		R
17 E	U	R	O	C	H	E	Q	U	E		18 F	R	E	E
		A		E		D		C		19 N		L		
20 P	I	N	K		21 T	E	L	E	V	I	S	I	O	22 N
R		G		23 P		S		D		N		E		A
24 O	M	E	L	E	T	T	E		25 L	E	A	R	N	T
C				N		R		26 R		T				U
27 E	A	28 T		29 C	H	I	N	E	S	E		30 W	A	R
S		O		I		A		N		E		H		A
31 S	W	O	L	L	E	N		32 T	I	N	F	O	I	L

TEST 85:

1. miss **2.** understand **3.** switch **4.** gloves **5.** country **6.** well **7.** savings **8.** weakness **9.** course **10.** work **11.** ground **12.** afternoon **13.** fall **14.** hospital **15.** next **16.** step **17.** left **18.** late **19.** wood **20.** good

TEST 86:

1. Money makes the world go round.
2. Never look a gift horse in the mouth.
3. No man is a prophet in his own country.
4. No rose without a thorn.
5. No sweet without sweat.
6. Old love never dies.
7. One does not wash one's dirty linen in public.
8. One hand washes the other.
9. One swallow does not make a summer.
10. Opportunity makes a thief.
11. Opposites attract.

12. Poverty is no sin.
13. Practice makes perfect.
14. Revenge is sweet.
15. Speak of the devil, and he is bound to appear.
16. Speech is silver but silence is golden.
17. Strike while the iron is hot.
18. The apple never falls far from the tree.
19. The bigger they are, the harder they fall.
20. The early bird catches the worm.

TEST 87:

1. Brazil
2. to see
3. tablecloth
4. modern
5. to freeze
6. Hungary
7. to cook
8. to burn
9. solid
10. month
11. fruit
12. sad
13. war
14. fish
15. hot
16. monk
17. melody
18. fun

TEST 88:

1. Make **2.** probably **3.** Sorry **4.** know **5.** enough **6.** chicken **7.** right **8.** more **9.** learn **10.** Open **11.** sold **12.** old **13.** cake **14.** tomorrow **15.** pace **16.** accept **17.** condition **18.** luggage **19.** letters **20.** Good

TEST 89:

1. ALBANIA **2.** AUSTRIA **3.** BELGIUM **4.** BOSNIA **5.** BULGARIA **6.** CROATIA **7.** CYPRUS **8.** DENMARK **9.** FINLAND **10.** FRANCE **11.** GERMANY **12.** GREECE **13.** HUNGARY **14.** ICELAND **15.** IRELAND **16.** LUXEMBOURG **17.** NETHERLANDS **18.** NORWAY **19.** POLAND **20.** PORTUGAL **21.** ROMANIA **22.** RUSSIA **23.** SLOVAKIA **24.** SLOVENIA **25.** SPAIN **26.** SWEDEN **27.** SWITZERLAND **28.** TURKEY **29.** YUGOSLAVIA

LÖSUNGEN

TEST 90:

1. hardworking - lazy
2. large / big - small
3. fat - thin
4. slow - fast
5. beautiful - ugly
6. near - far
7. dark - light
8. expensive - cheap
9. intelligent - stupid
10. white - black
11. soft - hard
12. many - few
13. alive - dead
14. exciting - boring
15. low - high
16. northern - southern
17. short - long
18. ill - healthy
19. single - married
20. right - left

TEST 91:

1. business **2.** How **3.** well **4.** at **5.** coat **6.** cross **7.** problem **8.** deserved **9.** pieces **10.** speak **11.** television **12.** into **13.** created **14.** there **15.** forbidden **16.** Turn **17.** bill **18.** holiday **19.** breath **20.** mood

TEST 92:

A young man in a French town claimed he was better at household chores than his wife. So she left him. He had to take care of things on his own. He learnt to iron, cook, clean and wash. One day he wanted to get rid of a particularly problematic stain on his clothes. He remembered that his mother had told him that gasoline cleans exceptionally well. So, he poured gasoline instead of washing powder into the washing machine. Then he went shopping. When he returned, his apartment had disappeared. A spark in the machine had caused an explosion which had burnt down the whole apartment. The stain was also gone.

TEST 93:

The lady who had the maximum number of children in Germany lived about 500 years ago. Her tombstone states that she gave birth to 38 boys and 15 girls, a total of 53 babies. This is not a high number when compared to a Russian farmer's wife who is supposed to have had 69 children, almost all of whom were born as quadruplets, triplets or twins. It is not known how many of them survived.

TEST 94:

1. directory **2.** allowed **3.** an **4.** cheque **5.** customers **6.** damaged **7.** skin **8.** Right **9.** working **10.** as **11.** seventy **12.** much **13.** help **14.** order **15.** sorry **16.** tomorrow **17.** anything **18.** Christmas **19.** anybody

TEST 95:

1. participants
2. Romania
3. colour
4. people
5. speech
6. blue
7. hate
8. calculate
9. penguin
10. beverage
11. roof
12. paint
13. chemical
14. floor
15. fish
16. intelligence
17. art
18. economic
19. cars
20. Slovakia

TEST 96:

1. WINDSURFING **2.** VOLLEYBALL **3.** WRESTLING **4.** BILLIARDS **5.** BADMINTON **6.** SWIMMING **7.** SHOOTING **8.** HURDLING **9.** HANDBALL **10.** FOOTBALL **11.** SAILING **12.** GLIDING **13.** BOWLING **14.** FENCING **15.** SKATING **16.** SKIING **17.** TENNIS **18.** DIVING **19.** ROWING **20.** RIDING **21.** KARATE **22.** HOCKEY **23.** BOXING **24.** CHESS **25.** POLO **26.** JUDO **27.** GOLF

TEST 97:

1. nine **2.** discussion **3.** without **4.** in **5.** first **6.** think **7.** night **8.** country **9.** piece **10.** breakdown **11.** roll **12.** can **13.** has **14.** bear **15.** banks **16.** pretending **17.** languages **18.** store **19.** clock **20.** way

L Ö S U N G E N

TEST 98:

1. The exception proves the rule.
2. The leopard cannot change its spots.
3. The love of money is the root of all evil.
4. The road to hell is paved with good intentions.
5. The shoemaker's son always goes barefoot.
6. The sun shines upon all alike.
7. The tree is known by its fruit.
8. There are two sides to everything.
9. Time is money.
10. To err is human.
11. Too many cooks spoil the broth.
12. We all have our cross to bear.
13. Well begun is half done.
14. When in Rome, do as the Romans do.
15. When the cat's away the mice will play.
16. Where there is smoke there's fire.
17. Where there's a will there's a way.
18. You can't see the forest for the trees.
19. You can't have your cake and eat it.
20. You can't make an omelette without breaking eggs.

TEST 99:

1. whisper **2.** bellow **3.** drink **4.** speak **5.** snore **6.** smile **7.** laugh **8.** cough **9.** spit **10.** sing **11.** suck **12.** call **13.** kiss **14.** chew **15.** yawn **16.** blow **17.** bite **18.** eat

TEST 100:

1. fish **2.** directions **3.** blocked **4.** took **5.** insurance **6.** look **7.** wants **8.** receipt **9.** brother **10.** leg **11.** comfortable **12.** touch **13.** find **14.** connected **15.** matters **16.** tell **17.** boring **18.** translation **19.** temper **20.** soon

Teil 2

Georgina Hodge

Verbtabellen Englisch

Die wichtigsten regelmäßigen und unregelmäßigen Verben im Überblick

Inhalt

Vorwort

Verbtabellen Englisch bietet die **wichtigsten regelmäßigen und unregelmäßigen Verben** zum Lernen und Nachschlagen. Das Werk richtet sich an Englischlernende aller Stufen, vom Anfänger bis zum Fortgeschrittenen. Es eignet sich zum Selbststudium, kann aber auch kursbegleitend eingesetzt werden.

Verbtabellen Englisch ist **übersichtlich** gestaltet. Jedem Verb ist eine eigene Seite gewidmet, auf der **umfassend** alle Zeiten des Verbs – einfache Formen und Verlaufsform – dargestellt werden.

Verbtabellen Englisch enthält insgesamt **75 Konjugationstabellen der gebräuchlichsten regelmäßigen und unregelmäßigen Verben** in alphabetischer Reihenfolge. Hinzu kommt je eine Tabelle zur Bildung der **Passivformen** und der **reflexiven Verben** sowie eine Übersicht über die wichtigsten **unregelmäßigen Verben** des Englischen.

Verbtabellen Englisch bietet darüber hinaus:

- Eine Übersicht über die wichtigsten **grammatischen Fachbegriffe** im Englischen und Deutschen.
- Eine **Einführung** mit Hinweisen zur Aussprache, zur Schreibung, zu Unterschieden zwischen britischem und amerikanischem Englisch sowie zur Bildung und zum Gebrauch aller Zeitformen mit Beispielsätzen und deutscher Übersetzung.
- Nützliche **Lerntipps** zum effizienten und gezielten Üben der Verbformen.

Hinweise zum Gebrauch der Verbtabellen

Die Verben in den Verbtabellen sind alphabetisch geordnet.

Erklärung des Aufbaus der Verbtabellen:

write [raɪt] *schreiben* — 1

Present — 2

5		Present simple	Present continuous	Present perfect simple	Present perfect continuous
	I	write	am wri**ting**	have **written**	have been wri**ting**
	you	write	are wri**ting**	have **written**	have been wri**ting**
5	he/she/it	write**s**	is wri**ting**	has **written**	has been wri**ting**
	we	write	are wri**ting**	have **written**	have been wri**ting**
	you	write	are wri**ting**	have **written**	have been wri**ting**
	they	write	are wri**ting**	have **written**	have been wri**ting**

4 3 4

Past

	Past simple	Past continuous	Past perfect simple	Past perfect continuous
I	**wrote**	was wri**ting**	had **written**	had been wri**ting**
you	**wrote**	were wri**ting**	had **written**	had been wri**ting**
he/she/it	**wrote**	was wri**ting**	had **written**	had been wri**ting**
we	**wrote**	were wri**ting**	had **written**	had been wri**ting**
you	**wrote**	were wri**ting**	had **written**	had been wri**ting**
they	**wrote**	were wri**ting**	had **written**	had been wri**ting**

4

Future

	Future simple	Future continuous	Future perfect simple	Future perfect continuous
I	will write	will be wri**ting**	will have **written**	will have been wri**ting**
you	will write	will be wri**ting**	will have **written**	will have been wri**ting**
he/she/it	will write	will be wri**ting**	will have **written**	will have been wri**ting**
we	will write	will be wri**ting**	will have **written**	will have been wri**ting**
you	will write	will be wri**ting**	will have **written**	will have been wri**ting**
they	will write	will be wri**ting**	will have **written**	will have been wri**ting**

4 4

Conditional

	Conditional	Conditional past
I	would write	would have **written**
you	would write	would have **written**
he/she/it	would write	would have **written**
we	would write	would have **written**
you	would write	would have **written**
they	would write	would have **written**

4

Imperative
write

Gerund
wri**ting** — 3

Past participle
written — 3

102

1 **Verb** in der Grundform (*infinitive*) mit Lautschrift und deutscher Übersetzung.

2 **Gliederung**

Sämtliche Verbtabellen gliedern sich in die Zeiten *present*, *past* und *future*. Jede dieser Zeiten ist wiederum in einfache Formen (*simple forms*) und Verlaufsformen (*continuous forms*) untergliedert. Es folgen die Formen des *conditional*, *imperative*, *gerund* und *past participle*. Auf die *continuous*-Formen des *conditional* wurde verzichtet, da diese wie die des *future* gebildet werden, aber selten gebraucht werden.

3 **Farbige Hervorhebung von Besonderheiten und Unregelmäßigkeiten**

Dazu zählen

- orthographische Besonderheiten: Wegfall eines auslautenden *-e* bei der *-ing*-Form, Konsonantverdopplung beim *past simple*, *past participle* und bei der *-ing*-Form sowie Verwandlung des *y* zu *i* beim *past simple* und *past participle* von Verben, deren Grundform auf einen Konsonanten + *-y* endet.
- das *-(e)s* der 3. Person Singular,
- unregelmäßige Formen des *past simple* und *past participle*.

4 **Vollformen**

In den Verbtabellen werden nur die Vollformen angegeben, wie es im schriftlichen Sprachgebrauch üblich ist. Die Kurzformen, die hauptsächlich im gesprochenen Englisch verwendet werden, finden Sie auf Seite 11–12 im Überblick.

5 **Personalpronomen**

Aus Gründen der Übersichtlichkeit werden die Personalpronomen (*I* = ich, *you* = du, *he/she/it* = er/sie/es, *we* = wir, *you* = ihr/Sie, *they* = sie) nur jeweils am linken Seitenrand angegeben. Selbstverständlich müssen sie vor jeder Zeitform gebraucht werden.

Grammatische Fachbegriffe

Übersicht über die gebräuchlichsten englischen und deutschen Grammatikbegriffe

englische Begriffe	deutsche Begriffe
active (voice)	Aktiv / Tätigkeitsform
auxiliary	Hilfsverb / Hilfszeitwort
conditional	Konditional I / Bedingungsform I
conditional past	Konditional II / Bedingungsform II
conjugation	Konjugation / Beugung des Zeitworts
continuous form	Verlaufsform
consonant	Konsonant / Mitlaut
future	Futur I / Zukunft
future perfect	Futur II / vollendete Zukunft
gerund	Gerundium
imperative	Imperativ / Befehlsform
infinitive	Infinitiv / Grundform des Verbs
irregular verb	unregelmäßiges Verb / Zeitwort
modal verb	Modalverb
participle	Partizip / Mittelwort
passive (voice)	Passiv / Leideform
past	Präteritum / Vergangenheit
past participle	Partizip Perfekt / Mittelwort der Vergangenheit
past perfect	Plusquamperfekt / vollendete Vergangenheit
personal pronoun	Personalpronomen / persönliches Fürwort
phrasal verb	zusammengesetztes Verb / Zeitwort
plural	Plural / Mehrzahl
predicate	Prädikat / Satzaussage
present	Präsens / Gegenwart
present perfect	Perfekt / vollendete Gegenwart
progressive form	Verlaufsform
pronoun	Pronomen / Fürwort
reflexive pronoun	Reflexivpronomen / rückbezügliches Fürwort
reflexive verb	reflexives Verb / rückbezügliches Zeitwort

englische Begriffe	deutsche Begriffe
regular verb	regelmäßiges Verb / Zeitwort
simple form	einfache Form
singular	Singular / Einzahl
subject	Subjekt / Satzgegenstand
tense	Tempus / Zeitform
verb	Verb / Zeitwort
vowel	Vokal / Selbstlaut

Lerntipps

1. Die wichtigsten Formen eines englischen Verbs sind die Grundform, das **simple past** und das **past participle**. Wenn Sie ein neues Verb lernen, sollten Sie sich diese Formen immer zuerst einprägen.

2. Wenn Sie die Konjugation eines Verbs üben wollen, empfiehlt es sich, dies vorher mehrmals schriftlich zu tun. Sie werden sehen, wie leicht sich die Formen dann einprägen. Dabei sprechen Sie die Verbformen, die Sie schreiben, laut nach.

3. Wenn Sie einen Lernpartner haben, können Sie zu zweit die Konjugationen üben. Fragen Sie sich gegenseitig und abwechselnd die unregelmäßigen Verben ab. Zuerst geben Sie die Grundform vor und Ihr Lernpartner bildet das **simple past** und das **past participle**. Sie sagen z. B.: **take**, Ihr Lernpartner sagt: **took, taken**. Versuchen Sie, dabei die Geschwindigkeit zu erhöhen. Oder konjugieren Sie zusammen ein Verb durch, eine Verbform nach der anderen, beispielsweise das **present**, zuerst immer die **simple**-Form, dann die **continuous**-Form, z. B. von **sleep**. Sie sagen: **I sleep**, **you sleep**, **he/she/it sleeps**, usw.; Ihr Lernpartner sagt: **I am sleeping**, **you are sleeping**, **he/she/it is sleeping**, usw.; Sie sagen: **I have slept**, **you have slept**, **he/she/it has slept**, usw. Dann dasselbe im **past** usw.

4. Sie können die Verbformen auch spielerisch üben. Nehmen Sie einen Spielwürfel. Die Zahlen 1–6 stehen jeweils für 1 = **present**, 2 = **past**, 3 = **future**, 4 = **conditional**, 5 = **gerund**, 6 = **participle** und für die Subjektpronomen: 1 = **I**, 2 = **you**, 3 = **he/she/it**, 4 = **we**, 5 = **you**, 6 = **they**. Sie wollen z. B. das Verb **eat** üben. Sie würfeln zwei Mal. Die erste Zahl entscheidet darüber, welche Zeitform Sie konjugieren sollen, die zweite Zahl bestimmt das Subjektpronomen, das Sie benutzen sollen. Ein Beispiel: Sie würfeln zuerst die 3, dann die 1. Sie konjugieren: **I will eat**, **I will be eating**, **I will have eaten**, **I will have been eating**.

Frage und Verneinung

Je nachdem, ob es sich um ein **Vollverb** oder um ein **Hilfs-** bzw. **Modalverb** handelt, werden Fragesätze und verneinte Sätze im Englischen unterschiedlich gebildet:

a. Vollverben (außer das Verb **be**, → **b**) werden mit dem Verb **do** umschrieben.

- Im **present simple** wird **do** bzw. **does** verwendet:

Aussagesatz	Fragesatz	verneinter Satz
You **work** a lot.	**Do** you **work** a lot?	You **do not/don't work** a lot.
He **works** a lot.	**Does** he **work** a lot?	He **does not/doesn't work** a lot.

Beachten Sie: Da das Verb in der Grundform angeschlossen wird, entfällt das **-s** der 3. Person Singular im **present simple**, also nicht: ~~Does he works a lot?~~

- Im **past simple** wird **did** verwendet:

Aussagesatz	Fragesatz	verneinter Satz
You **worked** a lot.	**Did** you **work** a lot?	You **did not/didn't work** a lot.

- Da alle anderen Zeiten mit Hilfsverben (**have**, **be**, **will** oder **would**) gebildet werden, werden Frage- und verneinte Sätze in diesen Zeiten nicht mit **do** umschrieben (→ **b**).

b. Sätze mit **Hilfs-** und **Modalverben** sowie das Vollverb **be** werden – wie im Deutschen – durch Inversion (Umstellung von Subjekt und Verb) zu Fragesätzen, bei der Verneinung steht **not** direkt hinter dem Verb, z. B.:

Aussagesatz	Fragesatz	verneinter Satz
You **are** a teacher.	**Are** you a teacher?	You **are not/aren't** a teacher.
You **have worked** a lot.	**Have** you **worked** a lot?	You **have not/haven't worked** a lot.
We **should** open the window.	**Should** we open the window?	We **should not** open the window.

Kurzformen

In den Verbtabellen werden immer die **Vollformen** angegeben, die im geschriebenen Englisch üblicherweise verwendet werden. In der gesprochenen Sprache sind jedoch in der Regel die **Kurzformen** gebräuchlich. **Verneinte Kurzformen** sind immer öfter auch im geschriebenen Englisch zu finden. Die folgende Tabelle gibt Ihnen einen Überblick über die gebräuchlichsten Kurzformen.

I am	→ I'm	I am not	→ I'm not
you are	→ you're	you are not	→ you're not / you aren't
he/she/it is	→ he's/she's/it's	he/she/it is not	→ he's/she's/he's not he/she/it isn't
we are	→ we're	we are not	→ we're not / we aren't
you are	→ you're	you are not	→ you're not / you aren't
they are	→ they're	they are not	→ they're not / they aren't
I have	→ I've	I have not	→ I've not / I haven't
you have	→ you've	you have not	→ you've not / you haven't
he/she/it has	→ he's/she's/it's	he/she/it has not	→ he's/she's/it's not / he/she/it hasn't
we have	→ we've	we have not	→ we've not / we haven't
you have	→ you've	you have not	→ you've not / you haven't
they have	→ they've	they have not	→ they've not / they haven't
I had	→ I'd	I had not	→ I'd not / I hadn't
you had	→ you'd	you had not	→ you'd not / you hadn't
he/she/it had	→ he'd/she'd/it'd	he/she/it had not	→ he'd/she'd/it'd not / he/she/it hadn't
we had	→ we'd	we had not	→ we'd not / we hadn't
you had	→ you'd	you had not	→ you'd not / you hadn't
they had	→ they'd	they had not	→ they'd not / they hadn't
I will	→ I'll	I will not	→ I'll not / I won't
you will	→ you'll	you will not	→ you'll not / you won't
he/she/it will	→ he'll/she'll/it'll	he/she/it will not	→ he'll/she'll/it'll not / he/she/it won't
we will	→ we'll	we will not	→ we'll not / we won't
you will	→ you'll	you will not	→ you'll not / you won't
they will	→ they'll	they will not	→ they'll not / they won't

I would	→ I'd
you would	→ you'd
he/she/it would	→ he'd/she'd/it'd
we would	→ we'd
you would	→ you'd
they would	→ they'd

I would not	→ I'd not / I wouldn't
you would not	→ you'd not / you wouldn't
he/she/it would not	→ he'd/she'd/it'd not / he/she/it wouldn't
we would not	→ we'd not / we wouldn't
you would not	→ you'd not / you wouldn't
they would not	→ they'd not / they wouldn't

I cannot	→ I can't
you cannot	→ you can't
he/she/it cannot	→ he/she/it can't
we cannot	→ we can't
you cannot	→ you can't
they cannot	→ they can't

I do not	→ I don't
you do not	→ you don't
he/she/it does not	→ he/she/it doesn't
we do not	→ we don't
you do not	→ you don't
they do not	→ they don't

I did not	→ I didn't
you did not	→ you didn't
he/she/it did not	→ he/she/it didn't
we did not	→ we didn't
you did not	→ you didn't
they did not	→ they didn't

I was not	→ I wasn't
you were not	→ you weren't
he/she/it was not	→ he/she/it wasn't
we were not	→ we weren't
you were not	→ you weren't
they were not	→ they weren't

Bildung und Gebrauch der Zeitformen

Man unterscheidet im Englischen 8 Zeiten, von denen es jeweils eine **simple form** (= einfache Form) und eine **continuous form** (= Verlaufsform, auch **progressive form** genannt) gibt. Die Kurzformen entnehmen Sie bitte der Tabelle auf S. 11–12.

a. Present simple

Die Formen des **present simple** sind mit der Grundform des Verbs identisch. In der 3. Person Singular wird an die Grundform **-s** bzw. **-es** angehängt (siehe auch → Besonderheiten in der Aussprache und → Besonderheiten in der Schreibung). Fragen und verneinte Sätze werden mit dem Hilfsverb **do** gebildet.

Aussagesatz		Fragesatz			Verneinung		
I	work	Do	I	work?	I	do not	work
you	work	Do	you	work?	you	do not	work
he/she/it	works	Does	he/she/it	work?	he/she/it	does not	work
we	work	Do	we	work?	we	do not	work
you	work	Do	you	work?	you	do not	work
they	work	Do	they	work?	they	do not	work

Das **present simple** wird für Dauerzustände, Eigenschaften, Gewohnheiten, regelmäßige Vorgänge sowie für Erzählungen gebraucht. Beispiele:

Water freezes at 0° celsius. — *Wasser gefriert bei 0° Celsius.*
Alice cooks really well. — *Alice kocht wirklich gut.*
Mark plays golf every Saturday. — *Mark spielt jeden Samstag Golf.*

b. Present continuous

Das **present continuous** wird folgendermaßen gebildet: **present simple** des Hilfsverbs **be** (= **am/are/is**) + **-ing**-Form des Verbs.

Aussagesatz		Fragesatz		Verneinung	
I	am working	Am I	working?	I	am not working
you	are working	Are you	working?	you	are not working
he/she/it	is working	Is he/she/it	working?	he/she/it	is not working
we	are working	Are we	working?	we	are not working
you	are working	Are you	working?	you	are not working
they	are working	Are they	working?	they	are not working

Das **present continuous** wird verwendet für im Moment des Sprechens ablaufende Handlungen, die noch im Gange, d.h. nicht abgeschlossen sind, sowie für vorübergehende Situationen. Das **present continuous** wird außerdem für fest geplante zukünftige Handlungen – in der Regel mit einer Zeitbestimmung – gebraucht. Bsp.:

I am having dinner now. — *Ich esse gerade zu Abend.*
Can I call you back later? — *Kann ich dich/Sie später zurückrufen?*
Thomas is living in London until he finishes his degree course. — *Thomas wird bis zum Ende seines Studiums in London leben.*
We're going skiing this winter. — *Wir gehen diesen Winter zum Skifahren.*

c. Present perfect simple

Das **present perfect simple** wird mit dem **present simple** des Hilfsverbs **have** und dem **past participle** des Hauptverbs gebildet. Das **past participle** der regelmäßigen Verben wird gebildet, indem man **-ed** an die Grundform des Verbs anhängt. Die unregelmäßigen Formen finden Sie auf den Seiten 103–108.

Aussagesatz		**Fragesatz**		**Verneinung**	
I	have worked	Have I	worked?	I	have not worked
you	have worked	Have you	worked?	you	have not worked
he/she/it	has worked	Has he/she/it	worked?	he/she/it	has not worked
we	have worked	Have we	worked?	we	have not worked
you	have worked	Have you	worked?	you	have not worked
they	have worked	Have they	worked?	they	have not worked

Das **present perfect simple** wird für Handlungen gebraucht, die in der Vergangenheit begonnen haben, die bzw. deren Auswirkungen aber bis in die Gegenwart reichen. Es wird außerdem verwendet, wenn der Zeitpunkt, zu dem die Handlung in der Vergangenheit stattgefunden hat, nicht genannt ist bzw. keine Rolle spielt. Oft wird es daher mit Zeitadverbien wie **already**, **so far**, **before**, **ever**, **never**, **yet** usw. gebraucht. Beispiele:

I haven't seen you here before.	*Ich habe dich/Sie hier noch nicht gesehen.*
Have you done your homework yet?	*Hast du deine Hausaufgaben schon gemacht?*
We have never been to Greece before, actually.	*Wir sind noch nie in Griechenland gewesen.*

d. Present perfect continuous

Das **present perfect continuous** wird folgendermaßen gebildet: **present perfect simple** des Hilfsverbs **be** (= **have/has been**) + **-ing**-Form des Verbs.

Aussagesatz		**Fragesatz**	
I	have been working	Have I	been working?
you	have been working	Have you	been working?
he/she/it	has been working	Has he/she/it	been working?
we	have been working	Have we	been working?
you	have been working	Have you	been working?
they	have been working	Have they	been working?

Verneinung	
I	have not been working
you	have not been working
he/she/it	has not been working
we	have not been working
you	have not been working
they	have not been working

Wie das **present perfect simple** wird das **present perfect continuous** für Handlungen verwendet, die bis in die Gegenwart reichen. Die **continuous**-Form betont das Andauern der Handlungen. Beispiele:

He has been studying all night.	*Er hat die ganze Nacht gelernt.*
I don't think that you have been listening to me, have you?	*Ich glaube nicht, dass du/Sie mir zugehört hast/haben, nicht wahr?*
We have not been working on this project for very long.	*Wir arbeiten noch nicht sehr lange an diesem Projekt.*

e. Past simple

Das **Past simple** der regelmäßigen Verben wird gebildet, indem man die Endung **-ed** an die Grundform des Verbs anhängt (siehe auch → Besonderheiten in der Aussprache und → Besonderheiten in der Schreibung). Die unregelmäßigen Verben finden Sie auf den Seiten 103–108. Fragen und verneinte Sätze werden mit dem Hilfsverb **did** gebildet.

Aussagesatz		**Fragesatz**		**Verneinung**	
I	worked	Did I	work?	I	did not work
you	worked	Did you	work?	you	did not work
he/she/it	worked	Did he/she/it	work?	he/she/it	did not work
we	worked	Did we	work?	we	did not work
you	worked	Did you	work?	you	did not work
they	worked	Did they	work?	they	did not work

Das **past simple** wird benutzt für abgeschlossene Handlungen, die zu/in einem explizit genannten oder gedachten Zeitpunkt/Zeitraum in der Vergangenheit stattgefunden haben. Oft wird es daher im Zusammenhang mit Zeitbestimmungen wie **yesterday**, **last year**, **in 1995**, **two weeks ago** usw. gebraucht. Es wird außerdem in irrealen Bedingungssätzen, die sich auf die Gegenwart oder Zukunft beziehen, gebraucht. Beispiele:

I saw a great film yesterday.	*Ich habe gestern einen tollen Film gesehen.*
We got married in 2002.	*Wir heirateten 2002.*
If I knew him better, I would share the flat with him.	*Wenn ich ihn besser kennen würde, würde ich mit ihm zusammen wohnen.*

f. Past continuous

Das **past continuous** wird folgendermaßen gebildet: **past simple** des Hilfsverbs **be** (= **was/were**) + **-ing**-Form des Verbs.

Aussagesatz		**Fragesatz**		**Verneinung**	
I	was working	Was I	working?	I	was not working
you	were working	Were you	working?	you	were not working
he/she/it	was working	Was he/she/it	working?	he/she/it	was not working
we	were working	Were we	working?	we	were not working
you	were working	Were you	working?	you	were not working
they	were working	Were they	working?	they	were not working

Das **past continuous** wird für Handlungen verwendet, die zu/in einem explizit genannten oder gedachten Zeitpunkt/Raumraum in der Vergangenheit im Verlauf begriffen waren. Beispiele:

I was listening to some music when the doorbell rang.	*Ich hörte gerade Musik, als es klingelte.*
We were living in Berlin at the time.	*Wir lebten damals in Berlin.*
Why were you looking at me like that?	*Warum hast du/haben Sie mich so angeschaut?*

g. Past perfect simple

Das **past perfect simple** wird mit **had** + **past participle** des Verbs gebildet. Die unregelmäßigen Formen des **past participle** finden Sie auf den Seiten 103–108.

Aussagesatz		Fragesatz		Verneinung	
I	had worked	Had I	worked?	I	had not worked
you	had worked	Had you	worked?	you	had not worked
he/she/it	had worked	Had he/she/it	worked?	he/she/it	had not worked
we	had worked	Had we	worked?	we	had not worked
you	had worked	Had you	worked?	you	had not worked
they	had worked	Had they	worked?	they	had not worked

Das **past perfect simple** wird verwendet für Handlungen, die vor anderen Handlungen in der Vergangenheit stattgefunden haben („Vorvergangenheit") und zu einem bestimmten Zeitpunkt bereits abgeschlossen waren. Es wird außerdem in irrealen Bedingungssätzen, die sich auf die Vergangenheit beziehen, gebraucht. Beispiele:

She called her lover after her husband had left for a business trip.	*Sie rief ihren Liebhaber an, nachdem ihr Mann auf eine Geschäftsreise gegangen war.*
If I had understood the problem, I wouldn't have made that mistake.	*Wenn ich das Problem verstanden hätte, hätte ich nicht diesen Fehler gemacht.*
I wish I had gone to the party. I heard it was fantastic.	*Ich wünschte, ich wäre auf die Party gegangen. Ich habe gehört, sie war fantastisch.*

h. Past perfect continuous

Das **past perfect continuous** wird folgendermaßen gebildet: **past perfect simple** des Hilfsverbs **be** (= **had been**) + **-ing**-Form des Verbs.

Aussagesatz		Fragesatz	
I	had been working	Had I	been working?
you	had been working	Had you	been working?
he/she/it	had been working	Had he/she/it	been working?
we	had been working	Had we	been working?
you	had been working	Had you	been working?
they	had been working	Had they	been working?

Verneinung	
I	had not been working
you	had not been working
he/she/it	had not been working
we	had not been working
you	had not been working
they	had not been working

Das **past perfect continuous** wird wie das **past perfect simple** für Handlungen verwendet, die vor anderen Handlungen in der Vergangenheit stattgefunden haben, betont aber deren Andauern. Beispiele:

I had been living in that village all my life. — *Ich hatte mein ganzes Leben in diesem Dorf gelebt.*

Had you not been sleeping so deeply, you would have heard the thunderstorm. — *Wenn du nicht so tief geschlafen hättest, hättest du das Gewitter gehört.*

We had not been planning on coming, but perhaps we will. — *Wir hatten nicht geplant zu kommen, aber vielleicht tun wir es.*

i. Future simple

Das **future simple** wird mit **will*** + Grundform des Verbs gebildet.

Aussagesatz		Fragesatz		Verneinung	
I	will work	Will I	work?	I	will not work
you	will work	Will you	work?	you	will not work
he/she/it	will work	Will he/she/it	work?	he/she/it	will not work
we	will work	Will we	work?	we are	will not work
you	will work	Will you	work?	you	will not work
they	will work	Will they	work?	they	will not work

Das **future simple** wird für zukünftige Handlungen (Vorhersagen, Annahmen über die Zukunft) und spontane Entschlüsse verwendet. Um Absicht, Entschlossenheit oder Gewissheit einer zukünftigen Handlung zu betonen, wird die Konstruktion **be going to** gebraucht. Auch mit dem → **present continuous** kann Zukünftigkeit ausgedrückt werden, wenn eine Handlung planmäßig in der Zukunft stattfinden wird. Beispiele:

It will rain tomorrow. — *Morgen wird es regnen.*

I will not stop until I have finished the job. — *Ich höre nicht auf, bis ich die Arbeit erledigt habe.*

Will you come along with me? I would love some company. — *Kommst du/Kommen Sie mit mir? Es wäre schön, wenn mich jemand begleiten würde.*

* Neben **will** wird auch **shall** verwendet (nur in der 1. Person Singular und Plural). **Shall** ist förmlicher als **will** und wird seltener benutzt, im amerikanischen Englisch kaum.

j. Future continuous

Das **future continuous** wird folgendermaßen gebildet: **future simple** des Hilfsverbs **be** (= **will* be**) + **-ing**-Form des Verbs.

Aussagesatz		Fragesatz	
I	will be working	Will I	be working?
you	will be working	Will you	be working?
he/she/it	will be working	Will he/she/it	be working?
we	will be working	Will we	be working?
you	will be working	Will you	be working?
they	will be working	Will they	be working?

Verneinung	
I	will not be working
you	will not be working
he/she/it	will not be working
we	will not be working
you	will not be working
they	will not be working

Das **future continuous** betont den Verlauf einer zukünftigen Handlung zu einem bestimmten Zeitpunkt. Es drückt außerdem eine planmäßig in der Zukunft ablaufende Handlung aus und wird verwendet, um höflich nach den Zukunftsplänen anderer zu fragen. Beispiele:

I will be travelling around Australia this time next year. — *Nächstes Jahr um diese Zeit werde ich durch Australien reisen.*

Will you be coming to see us at Christmas? — *Besuchst du/Besuchen Sie uns an Weihnachten?*

They will not be working on Monday. It's a Bank Holiday. — *Sie arbeiten nicht am Montag. Es ist ein Feiertag.*

k. Future perfect simple

Das **future perfect simple** wird mit **will* have** + **past participle** des Verbs gebildet. Die unregelmäßigen Formen des **past participle** finden Sie auf den Seiten 103–108.

Aussagesatz		Fragesatz	
I	will have worked	Will I	have worked?
you	will have worked	Will you	have worked?
he/she/it	will have worked	Will he/she/it	have worked?
we	will have worked	Will we	have worked?
you	will have worked	Will you	have worked?
they	will have worked	Will they	have worked?

* Neben **will** wird auch **shall** verwendet (nur in der 1. Person Singular und Plural). **Shall** ist förmlicher als **will** und wird seltener benutzt, im amerikanischen Englisch kaum.

Verneinung	
I	will not have worked
you	will not have worked
he/she/it	will not have worked
we	will not have worked
you	will not have worked
they	will not have worked

Das **future perfect simple** wird für Handlungen gebraucht, die vor anderen Handlungen in der Zukunft abgeschlossen sein werden („vollendete Zukunft").
Beispiele:

I will have finished the job by this evening.	*Ich werde die Arbeit bis heute Abend erledigt haben.*
We will have been married for five years in April.	*Im April werden wir fünf Jahre verheiratet sein.*

l. Future perfect continuous

Das **future perfect continuous** wird folgendermaßen gebildet: **future perfect simple** des Hilfsverbs **be** (= **will* have been**) + **-ing**-Form des Verbs.

Aussagesatz		Fragesatz	
I	will have been working	Will I	have been working?
you	will have been working	Will you	have been working?
he/she/it	will have been working	Will he/she/it	have been working?
we	will have been working	Will we	have been working?
you	will have been working	Will you	have been working?
they	will have been working	Will they	have been working?

Verneinung	
I	will not have been working
you	will not have been working
he/she/it	will not have been working
we	will not have been working
you	will not have been working
they	will not have been working

Wie das **future perfect simple** wird das **future perfect continuous** für Handlungen gebraucht, die vor anderen Handlungen in der Zukunft abgeschlossen sein werden („vollendete Zukunft"). Die **continuous**-Form betont das Andauern der Handlungen, wird aber selten verwendet. Beispiele:

Will they have been waiting for us all this time?	*Ob sie wohl die ganze Zeit auf uns gewartet haben (werden)?*
You know mum, she will have been cooking and baking all day.	*Du kennst ja Mutti, sie wird den ganzen Tag gekocht und gebacken haben.*

* Neben **will** wird auch **shall** verwendet (nur in der 1. Person Singular und Plural). **Shall** ist förmlicher als **will** und wird seltener benutzt, im amerikanischen Englisch kaum.

m. Conditional

Das **conditional** wird mit **would** + Grundform des Verbs gebildet.

Aussagesatz		Fragesatz		Verneinung	
I	would work	Would I	work?	I	would not work
you	would work	Would you	work?	you	would not work
he/she/it	would work	Would he/she/it	work?	he/she/it	would not work
we	would work	Would we	work?	we	would not work
you	would work	Would you	work?	you	would not work
they	would work	Would they	work?	they	would not work

Das **conditional** wird in irrealen Bedingungssätzen, die sich auf die Gegenwart oder Zukunft beziehen, und für höfliche Bitten und Fragen gebraucht. Es gibt auch eine **continuous**-Form des **conditional**, diese wird aber selten verwendet und wird deshalb in den Verbtabellen nicht erwähnt. Beispiele:

If I had my way, I wouldn't invite him. — *Wenn es nach mir ginge, würde ich ihn nicht einladen.*

I would work overtime if they paid us a bonus. — *Ich würde Überstunden machen, wenn Sie uns eine Prämie zahlen würden.*

Would you please open the window? — *Würdest du/Würden Sie bitte das Fenster aufmachen?*

n. Conditional past

Das **conditional past** wird mit **would have** + **past participle** des Verbs gebildet. Die unregelmäßigen Formen des **past participle** finden Sie auf den Seiten 103–108.

Aussagesatz		Fragesatz	
I	would have worked	Would I	have worked?
you	would have worked	Would you	have worked?
he/she/it	would have worked	Would he/she/it	have worked?
we	would have worked	Would we	have worked?
you	would have worked	Would you	have worked?
they	would have worked	Would they	have worked?

Verneinung	
I	would not have worked
you	would not have worked
he/she/it	would not have worked
we	would not have worked
you	would not have worked
they	would not have worked

Das **conditional past** wird in irrealen Bedingungssätzen gebraucht, die sich auf die Vergangenheit beziehen. Es gibt auch eine **continuous**-Form des **conditional past**, diese wird aber selten verwendet und wird deshalb in den Verbtabellen nicht erwähnt. Beispiele:

If she had liked it, I would have bought it.	*Wenn es ihr gefallen hätte, hätte ich es gekauft.*
I would have loved to come and see you, but I didn't have the time.	*Ich hätte dich/Sie sehr gern besucht, aber ich hatte keine Zeit.*
We wouldn't have gone to that restaurant had we known it would be so expensive.	*Wir wären nicht in dieses Restaurant gegangen, wenn wir gewusst hätten, dass es so teuer ist.*

Besonderheiten in der Aussprache

a. Aussprache des -(e)s der 3. Person Singular des present simple

Die Aussprache der Endung **-(e)s** hängt vom vorausgehenden Laut ab.

Nach den **stimmhaften** Konsonanten [b], [d], [g], [l], [m], [n], [ŋ], [v] und nach Vokalen: → Aussprache: **[z]** (Regelfall)	arrives runs knows	**[z]**	[ə'raɪv**z**] [rʌn**z**] [nəʊ**z**]
Nach den **stimmlosen** Konsonanten [p], [f], [k] und [t]: → Aussprache: **[s]**	stops sniffs looks gets	**[s]**	[stɒp**s**] [snɪf**s**] [lʊk**s**] [get**s**]
Nach den Konsonanten [s], [z], [ʃ], [tʃ] und [dʒ]: → Aussprache: **[ɪz]**	kisses looses wishes watches changes	**[ɪz]**	['kɪs**ɪz**] ['lu:z**ɪz**] ['wɪʃ**ɪz**] ['wɒtʃ**ɪz**] ['tʃeɪndʒ**ɪz**]
Ausnahmen: says [sez] nicht ~~[seɪz]~~ does [dʌz] nicht ~~[du:z]~~			

b. Aussprache des -ed im past simple bzw. past participle

Auch die Aussprache der Endung **-ed** hängt vom vorausgehenden Laut ab.

Nach den **stimmhaften** Konsonanten [b], [d], [g], [l], [m], [n], [ŋ], [v], [z], [dʒ] und nach Vokalen: → Aussprache: **[d]** (Regelfall)	earned dived changed tried	**[d]**	[ɜ:n**d**] [daɪv**d**] ['tʃeɪndʒ**d**] [traɪ**d**]
Nach den **stimmlosen** Konsonanten [p], [f], [k], [s] und [tʃ]: → Aussprache: **[t]**	helped laughed worked	**[t]**	[help**t**] [lɑ:f**t**] [wɜ:k**t**]
Nach **[d]** und **[t]**: → Aussprache: **[ɪd]**	ended started	**[ɪd]**	['end**ɪd**] ['stɑ:t**ɪd**]

Besonderheiten in der Schreibung

a. 3. Person Singular des present simple

Die meisten Verben hängen **-s** an die Grundform an: **Grundform + -s** (Regelfall)	sit → sit**s** stay → stay**s** work → work**s**
Bei Verben, die auf einen **Konsonanten** + **-y** enden, wird das **y** zu **i** und es wird **-es** angehängt: **y → i + es**	cry → cr**ies** hurry → hurr**ies** reply → repl**ies**
Verben, die auf **-s**, **-z**, **-ch**, **-sh** oder **-x** enden, hängen **-es** an die Grundform an: **Grundform + -es**	miss → miss**es** buzz → buzz**es** watch → watch**es** push → push**es** fix → fix**es**
Ausnahmen:	be → **is** do → do**es** go → go**es** have → ha**s**

b. Simple past bzw. past participle

Die meisten Verben hängen **-ed** an die Grundform an: **Grundform + -ed** (Regelfall)	work → work**ed** start → start**ed** stay → stay**ed**
Verben, die auf **-e** enden, hängen nur **-d** an die Grundform an: **Grundform ohne -e + -d**	arrive → arrive**d** decide → decide**d** hope → hope**d**
Bei Verben, die auf einen betonten (und in der Regel kurzen) **Vokal** + **Konsonanten** enden (Ausnahme: **w** und **y**), wird der Konsonant verdoppelt: **Konsonantverdopplung + -ed**	shop → sho**pp**ed plan → pla**nn**ed stop → sto**pp**ed prefer → prefe**rr**ed
Bei Verben, die auf einen **Konsonanten** + **-y** enden, wird das **y** zu **i** und es wird **-ed** angehängt: **y → i + -ed**	hurry → hurr**ied** cry → cr**ied** study → stud**ied**
Bei Verben, die auf **-c** enden, wird dieses zu **-ck** und es wird **-ed** angehängt: **Grundform auf -c → -ck + -ed**	panic → pani**ck**ed picnic → pini**ck**ed

c. **ing-Form**

Die meisten Verben hängen **-ing** an die Grundform an: **Grundform + -ing**	work start stay	→ → →	work**ing** start**ing** stay**ing**
Verben, die auf **-e** enden, verlieren das **-e**: **Grundform ohne -e + -ing** **Ausnahmen: die → dying, lie → lying, tie → tying**	arrive decide hope	→ → →	arri**ving** deci**ding** ho**ping**
Bei Verben, die auf einen betonten (und in der Regel kurzen) **Vokal + Konsonanten** enden (Ausnahme: **w** und **y**), wird der Konsonant verdoppelt: **Konsonantverdopplung + -ing**	shop plan stop prefer	→ → → →	sho**pp**ing pla**nn**ing sto**pp**ing prefe**rr**ing

Reflexive Verben

Reflexive Verben werden mit **Reflexivpronomen** (= rückbezügliche Fürwörter) gebildet. Diese stehen immer nach der jeweiligen Verbform, bei den zusammengesetzten Zeiten nach dem **past participle**, bei den **continuous**-Formen nach der **-ing**-Form.

Musterkonjugation eines reflexiven Verbs am Beispiel von **wash oneself** (*sich waschen*) im **present simple**:

I wash **myself**
you wash **yourself**
he/she/it washes **himself/herself/itself**
we wash **ourselves**
you wash **yourselves**
they wash **themselves**
neutrale Form: **oneself**

Modalverben

Die 10 Modalverben des Englischen sind:

can – could	*kann .../darf ... – konnte/könnte/dürfte ...*
may – might	*kann/darf ... – könnte/dürfte ...*
must	*muss .../(in verneinten Sätzen) darf ...*
ought to	*sollte ...*
shall – should	*wird ... – sollte/müsste ...*
will – would	*wird ... – würde ...*

Nach einem Modalverb folgt die Grundform des Hauptverbs. Modalverben drücken Fähigkeit, Erlaubnis, Notwendigkeit, Möglichkeit usw. aus. Sie weisen die folgenden Charakteristika auf:

a. Modalverben haben **kein -s** in der 3. Person Singular des **present simple**.

She **can** ride a bike.	*Sie kann radfahren.*
He **may** come to the party.	*Vielleicht kommt er zur Party.*

b. Modalverben haben unvollständige Formensätze. In der Regel werden sie nur im **present simple**, einige auch im **past simple**, gebraucht. Alle andere Zeiten einschließlich Grundform, **gerund** und **past participle** existieren nicht, also: ~~to must, musting, musted~~.

May I come in?	*Darf ich hereinkommen?*
We **could** not find the keys.	*Wir konnten die Schlüssel nicht finden.*
You **should** go and see a doctor.	*Du solltest zum Arzt gehen.*

c. Die fehlenden Formen der Modalverben wie **can**, **may** und **must** werden durch Umschreibungen mit **be able to**, **be allowed to** und **have to** ausgedrückt.

I would like **to be able to** swim like that.	*So möchte ich auch schwimmen können.*
She **wasn't able to** come.	*Sie konnte nicht kommen.*
We **were allowed to** leave early.	*Wir durften früh gehen.*
People **had to** work hard in those days.	*Damals mussten die Leute viel arbeiten.*
The teacher said I **had to** study.	*Der Lehrer sagte mir, ich müsste lernen.*

Unterschiede zwischen britischem und amerikanischem Englisch

Britisches Englisch (**British English = BE**) und amerikanisches Englisch (**American English = AE**) unterscheiden sich im Wesentlichen nur in der Aussprache und Schreibung. Hier sind die wichtigsten Unterschiede bezüglich der Verbformen.

a. Im AE wird in Verbindung mit den Zeitadverbien **just**, **already**, **yet**, **ever** und **never** häufig das **past simple** statt dem **present perfect** gebraucht.

BE	AE
He **has** just **gone** home.	He just **went** home.
I **have** never **heard** that.	I never **heard** that.

b. Orthographische Unterschiede: Im BE wird bei Verben, deren Grundform auf Vokal + **-l** oder **-r** endet, dieser Endkonsonant im **past simple** bzw. **past participle** verdoppelt, dasselbe gilt für die **-ing**-Form der Verben auf **-l**. Die Verb-Endung **-ise** (BE) wird im AE **-ize** geschrieben.

BE	AE
trave**ll**ed / trave**ll**ing	trave**l**ed / trave**l**ing
refe**rr**ed	refe**r**ed
critic**ise**	critic**ize**

c. Im mündlichen BE wird **have** häufig nicht als Vollverb gebraucht, sondern in der Form **have got**, im AE wird dagegen fast ausschließlich **have** benutzt, das bei Fragen und in der Verneinung mit **do** umschrieben wird.

BE	AE
I **have got** a younger sister.	I **have** a younger sister.
Have you **got** the time?	**Do** you **have** the time?

d. Einige Verben, die im BE unregelmäßig sind (oder sein können), sind im AE regelmäßig (oder werden auch regelmäßig gebraucht). Einige Verben haben im AE eine andere unregelmäßige Form als im BE. Die folgende Darstellung enthält jeweils: Grundform – **past simple** – **past participle**.

BE	AE
get – got – **got**	get – got – **gotten**
leap – **leapt** / leaped – **leapt** / leaped	leap – **leaped** – **leaped**
learn – **learnt** / learned – **learnt** / learned	learn – **learned** – **learned**
saw – sawed – **sawn**	saw – sawed – **sawed** / sawn
sew – sewed – **sewn**	sew – sewed – **sewed** / sewn
smell – **smelt** / smelled – **smelt** / smelled	smell – **smelled** – **smelled**
spell – **spelt** / spelled – **spelt** / spelled	spell – **spelled** – **spelled**
spit – spat – spat	spit – spat / **spit** – spat / **spit**
spoil – **spoilt** / spoiled – **spoilt** / spoiled	spoil – **spoiled** – **spoiled**
spring – sprang – sprung	spring – sprang / **sprung** – sprung
strike – struck – struck	strike – struck – struck / **stricken**

Musterkonjugation Passiv *(passive voice)*

Das Passiv wird mit einer Form des Hilfsverbs **be** + **past participle** des Verbs gebildet. Die unregelmäßigen Formen des **past participle** finden Sie auf den Seiten 103–108. In einem Aktivsatz wird der Urheber der Handlung hervorgehoben, in einem Passivsatz, was mit einer Person oder einer Sache geschieht.

be shown ['bi: 'ʃəʊn] *gezeigt werden*

Present

	Present simple	Present continuous	Present perfect simple*
I	am shown	am being shown	have been shown
you	are shown	are being shown	have been shown
he/she/it	is shown	is being shown	have been shown
we	are shown	are being shown	have been shown
you	are shown	are being shown	have been shown
they	are shown	are being shown	have been shown

* Das **present perfect continuous** wird selten gebraucht.

Past

	Past simple	Past continuous	Past perfect simple*
I	was shown	was being shown	had been shown
you	were shown	were being shown	had been shown
he/she/it	was shown	was being shown	had been shown
we	were shown	were being shown	had been shown
you	were shown	were being shown	had been shown
they	were shown	were being shown	had been shown

* Das **past perfect continuous** wird selten gebraucht.

Future

	Future simple	Future continuous	Future perfect simple*
I	will be shown	will be being shown	will have been shown
you	will be shown	will be being shown	will have been shown
he/she/it	will be shown	will be being shown	will have been shown
we	will be shown	will be being shown	will have been shown
you	will be shown	will be being shown	will have been shown
they	will be shown	will be being shown	will have been shown

* Das **future perfect continuous** wird selten gebraucht.

Conditional

	Conditional*	Conditional past*
I	would be shown	would have been shown
you	would be shown	would have been shown
he/she/it	would be shown	would have been shown
we	would be shown	would have been shown
you	would be shown	would have been shown
they	would be shown	would have been shown

Imperative
be shown
Gerund
being shown

* Das **conditional continuous** und das **conditional past continuous** werden selten gebraucht.

answer ['ɑ:nsə] *antworten*

Present

	Present simple	Present continuous	Present perfect simple	Present perfect continuous
I	answer	am answering	have answered	have been answering
you	answer	are answering	have answered	have been answering
he/she/it	answers	is answering	has answered	has been answering
we	answer	are answering	have answered	have been answering
you	answer	are answering	have answered	have been answering
they	answer	are answering	have answered	have been answering

Past

	Past simple	Past continuous	Past perfect simple	Past perfect continuous
I	answered	was answering	had answered	had been answering
you	answered	were answering	had answered	had been answering
he/she/it	answered	was answering	had answered	had been answering
we	answered	were answering	had answered	had been answering
you	answered	were answering	had answered	had been answering
they	answered	were answering	had answered	had been answering

Future

	Future simple	Future continuous	Future perfect simple	Future perfect continuous
I	will answer	will be answering	will have answered	will have been answering
you	will answer	will be answering	will have answered	will have been answering
he/she/it	will answer	will be answering	will have answered	will have been answering
we	will answer	will be answering	will have answered	will have been answering
you	will answer	will be answering	will have answered	will have been answering
they	will answer	will be answering	will have answered	will have been answering

Conditional

	Conditional	Conditional past
I	would answer	would have answered
you	would answer	would have answered
he/she/it	would answer	would have answered
we	would answer	would have answered
you	would answer	would have answered
they	would answer	would have answered

Imperative
answer

Gerund
answering

Past participle
answered

arrive [əˈraɪv] *ankommen*

Present

	Present simple	Present continuous	Present perfect simple	Present perfect continuous
I	arrive	am arriving	have arrived	have been arriving
you	arrive	are arriving	have arrived	have been arriving
he/she/it	arrives	is arriving	has arrived	has been arriving
we	arrive	are arriving	have arrived	have been arriving
you	arrive	are arriving	have arrived	have been arriving
they	arrive	are arriving	have arrived	have been arriving

Past

	Past simple	Past continuous	Past perfect simple	Past perfect continuous
I	arrived	was arriving	had arrived	had been arriving
you	arrived	were arriving	had arrived	had been arriving
he/she/it	arrived	was arriving	had arrived	had been arriving
we	arrived	were arriving	had arrived	had been arriving
you	arrived	were arriving	had arrived	had been arriving
they	arrived	were arriving	had arrived	had been arriving

Future

	Future simple	Future continuous	Future perfect simple	Future perfect continuous
I	will arrive	will be arriving	will have arrived	will have been arriving
you	will arrive	will be arriving	will have arrived	will have been arriving
he/she/it	will arrive	will be arriving	will have arrived	will have been arriving
we	will arrive	will be arriving	will have arrived	will have been arriving
you	will arrive	will be arriving	will have arrived	will have been arriving
they	will arrive	will be arriving	will have arrived	will have been arriving

Conditional

	Conditional	Conditional past
I	would arrive	would have arrived
you	would arrive	would have arrived
he/she/it	would arrive	would have arrived
we	would arrive	would have arrived
you	would arrive	would have arrived
they	would arrive	would have arrived

Imperative
arrive

Gerund
arriving

Past participle
arrived

ask [ɑːsk] *fragen*

Present

	Present simple	Present continuous	Present perfect simple	Present perfect continuous
I	ask	am asking	have asked	have been asking
you	ask	are asking	have asked	have been asking
he/she/it	asks	is asking	has asked	has been asking
we	ask	are asking	have asked	have been asking
you	ask	are asking	have asked	have been asking
they	ask	are asking	have asked	have been asking

Past

	Past simple	Past continuous	Past perfect simple	Past perfect continuous
I	asked	was asking	had asked	had been asking
you	asked	were asking	had asked	had been asking
he/she/it	asked	was asking	had asked	had been asking
we	asked	were asking	had asked	had been asking
you	asked	were asking	had asked	had been asking
they	asked	were asking	had asked	had been asking

Future

	Future simple	Future continuous	Future perfect simple	Future perfect continuous
I	will ask	will be asking	will have asked	will have been asking
you	will ask	will be asking	will have asked	will have been asking
he/she/it	will ask	will be asking	will have asked	will have been asking
we	will ask	will be asking	will have asked	will have been asking
you	will ask	will be asking	will have asked	will have been asking
they	will ask	will be asking	will have asked	will have been asking

Conditional

	Conditional	Conditional past
I	would ask	would have asked
you	would ask	would have asked
he/she/it	would ask	would have asked
we	would ask	would have asked
you	would ask	would have asked
they	would ask	would have asked

Imperative
ask

Gerund
asking

Past participle
asked

be [bi:] *sein*

Present

	Present simple	Present continuous	Present perfect simple	Present perfect continuous
I	am	am being	have been	have been being
you	are	are being	have been	have been being
he/she/it	is	is being	has been	has been being
we	are	are being	have been	have been being
you	are	are being	have been	have been being
they	are	are being	have been	have been being

Past

	Past simple	Past continuous	Past perfect simple	Past perfect continuous
I	was	was being	had been	had been being
you	were	were being	had been	had been being
he/she/it	was	was being	had been	had been being
we	were	were being	had been	had been being
you	were	were being	had been	had been being
they	were	were being	had been	had been being

Future

	Future simple	Future continuous	Future perfect simple	Future perfect continuous
I	will be	will be being	will have been	will have been being
you	will be	will be being	will have been	will have been being
he/she/it	will be	will be being	will have been	will have been being
we	will be	will be being	will have been	will have been being
you	will be	will be being	will have been	will have been being
they	will be	will be being	will have been	will have been being

Conditional

	Conditional	Conditional past
I	would be	would have been
you	would be	would have been
he/she/it	would be	would have been
we	would be	would have been
you	would be	would have been
they	would be	would have been

Imperative
be

Gerund
being

Past participle
been

become [bɪ'kʌm] *werden*

Present

	Present simple	Present continuous	Present perfect simple	Present perfect continuous
I	become	am becoming	have become	have been becoming
you	become	are becoming	have become	have been becoming
he/she/it	becomes	is becoming	has become	has been becoming
we	become	are becoming	have become	have been becoming
you	become	are becoming	have become	have been becoming
they	become	are becoming	have become	have been becoming

Past

	Past simple	Past continuous	Past perfect simple	Past perfect continuous
I	became	was becoming	had become	had been becoming
you	became	were becoming	had become	had been becoming
he/she/it	became	was becoming	had become	had been becoming
we	became	were becoming	had become	had been becoming
you	became	were becoming	had become	had been becoming
they	became	were becoming	had become	had been becoming

Future

	Future simple	Future continuous	Future perfect simple	Future perfect continuous
I	will become	will be becoming	will have become	will have been becoming
you	will become	will be becoming	will have become	will have been becoming
he/she/it	will become	will be becoming	will have become	will have been becoming
we	will become	will be becoming	will have become	will have been becoming
you	will become	will be becoming	will have become	will have been becoming
they	will become	will be becoming	will have become	will have been becoming

Conditional

	Conditional	Conditional past
I	would become	would have become
you	would become	would have become
he/she/it	would become	would have become
we	would become	would have become
you	would become	would have become
they	would become	would have become

Imperative
become

Gerund
becoming

Past participle
become

begin [bɪ'gɪn] *beginnen, anfangen*

Present

	Present simple	Present continuous	Present perfect simple	Present perfect continuous
I	begin	am beginning	have **begun**	have been beginning
you	begin	are beginning	have **begun**	have been beginning
he/she/it	begins	is beginning	has **begun**	has been beginning
we	begin	are beginning	have **begun**	have been beginning
you	begin	are beginning	have **begun**	have been beginning
they	begin	are beginning	have **begun**	have been beginning

Past

	Past simple	Past continuous	Past perfect simple	Past perfect continuous
I	**began**	was beginning	had **begun**	had been beginning
you	**began**	were beginning	had **begun**	had been beginning
he/she/it	**began**	was beginning	had **begun**	had been beginning
we	**began**	were beginning	had **begun**	had been beginning
you	**began**	were beginning	had **begun**	had been beginning
they	**began**	were beginning	had **begun**	had been beginning

Future

	Future simple	Future continuous	Future perfect simple	Future perfect continuous
I	will begin	will be beginning	will have **begun**	will have been beginning
you	will begin	will be beginning	will have **begun**	will have been beginning
he/she/it	will begin	will be beginning	will have **begun**	will have been beginning
we	will begin	will be beginning	will have **begun**	will have been beginning
you	will begin	will be beginning	will have **begun**	will have been beginning
they	will begin	will be beginning	will have **begun**	will have been beginning

Conditional

	Conditional	Conditional past
I	would begin	would have **begun**
you	would begin	would have **begun**
he/she/it	would begin	would have **begun**
we	would begin	would have **begun**
you	would begin	would have **begun**
they	would begin	would have **begun**

Imperative
begin

Gerund
beginning

Past participle
begun

break [breɪk] *(zer)brechen*

Present

	Present simple	Present continuous	Present perfect simple	Present perfect continuous
I	break	am breaking	have broken	have been breaking
you	break	are breaking	have broken	have been breaking
he/she/it	breaks	is breaking	has broken	has been breaking
we	break	are breaking	have broken	have been breaking
you	break	are breaking	have broken	have been breaking
they	break	are breaking	have broken	have been breaking

Past

	Past simple	Past continuous	Past perfect simple	Past perfect continuous
I	broke	was breaking	had broken	had been breaking
you	broke	were breaking	had broken	had been breaking
he/she/it	broke	was breaking	had broken	had been breaking
we	broke	were breaking	had broken	had been breaking
you	broke	were breaking	had broken	had been breaking
they	broke	were breaking	had broken	had been breaking

Future

	Future simple	Future continuous	Future perfect simple	Future perfect continuous
I	will break	will be breaking	will have broken	will have been breaking
you	will break	will be breaking	will have broken	will have been breaking
he/she/it	will break	will be breaking	will have broken	will have been breaking
we	will break	will be breaking	will have broken	will have been breaking
you	will break	will be breaking	will have broken	will have been breaking
they	will break	will be breaking	will have broken	will have been breaking

Conditional

	Conditional	Conditional past
I	would break	would have broken
you	would break	would have broken
he/she/it	would break	would have broken
we	would break	would have broken
you	would break	would have broken
they	would break	would have broken

Imperative
break

Gerund
breaking

Past participle
broken

bring [brɪŋ] *bringen*

Present

	Present simple	Present continuous	Present perfect simple	Present perfect continuous
I	bring	am bringing	have **brought**	have been bringing
you	bring	are bringing	have **brought**	have been bringing
he/she/it	bring**s**	is bringing	has **brought**	has been bringing
we	bring	are bringing	have **brought**	have been bringing
you	bring	are bringing	have **brought**	have been bringing
they	bring	are bringing	have **brought**	have been bringing

Past

	Past simple	Past continuous	Past perfect simple	Past perfect continuous
I	**brought**	was bringing	had **brought**	had been bringing
you	**brought**	were bringing	had **brought**	had been bringing
he/she/it	**brought**	was bringing	had **brought**	had been bringing
we	**brought**	were bringing	had **brought**	had been bringing
you	**brought**	were bringing	had **brought**	had been bringing
they	**brought**	were bringing	had **brought**	had been bringing

Future

	Future simple	Future continuous	Future perfect simple	Future perfect continuous
I	will bring	will be bringing	will have **brought**	will have been bringing
you	will bring	will be bringing	will have **brought**	will have been bringing
he/she/it	will bring	will be bringing	will have **brought**	will have been bringing
we	will bring	will be bringing	will have **brought**	will have been bringing
you	will bring	will be bringing	will have **brought**	will have been bringing
they	will bring	will be bringing	will have **brought**	will have been bringing

Conditional

	Conditional	Conditional past
I	would bring	would have **brought**
you	would bring	would have **brought**
he/she/it	would bring	would have **brought**
we	would bring	would have **brought**
you	would bring	would have **brought**
they	would bring	would have **brought**

Imperative
bring

Gerund
bringing

Past participle
brought

buy [baɪ] *kaufen*

Present

	Present simple	Present continuous	Present perfect simple	Present perfect continuous
I	buy	am buying	have **bought**	have been buying
you	buy	are buying	have **bought**	have been buying
he/she/it	buy**s**	is buying	has **bought**	has been buying
we	buy	are buying	have **bought**	have been buying
you	buy	are buying	have **bought**	have been buying
they	buy	are buying	have **bought**	have been buying

Past

	Past simple	Past continuous	Past perfect simple	Past perfect continuous
I	**bought**	was buying	had **bought**	had been buying
you	**bought**	were buying	had **bought**	had been buying
he/she/it	**bought**	was buying	had **bought**	had been buying
we	**bought**	were buying	had **bought**	had been buying
you	**bought**	were buying	had **bought**	had been buying
they	**bought**	were buying	had **bought**	had been buying

Future

	Future simple	Future continuous	Future perfect simple	Future perfect continuous
I	will buy	will be buying	will have **bought**	will have been buying
you	will buy	will be buying	will have **bought**	will have been buying
he/she/it	will buy	will be buying	will have **bought**	will have been buying
we	will buy	will be buying	will have **bought**	will have been buying
you	will buy	will be buying	will have **bought**	will have been buying
they	will buy	will be buying	will have **bought**	will have been buying

Conditional

	Conditional	Conditional past
I	would buy	would have **bought**
you	would buy	would have **bought**
he/she/it	would buy	would have **bought**
we	would buy	would have **bought**
you	would buy	would have **bought**
they	would buy	would have **bought**

Imperative
buy

Gerund
buying

Past participle
bought

carry ['kæri] *tragen*

Present

	Present simple	Present continuous	Present perfect simple	Present perfect continuous
I	carry	am carrying	have carried	have been carrying
you	carry	are carrying	have carried	have been carrying
he/she/it	carries	is carrying	has carried	has been carrying
we	carry	are carrying	have carried	have been carrying
you	carry	are carrying	have carried	have been carrying
they	carry	are carrying	have carried	have been carrying

Past

	Past simple	Past continuous	Past perfect simple	Past perfect continuous
I	carried	was carrying	had carried	had been carrying
you	carried	were carrying	had carried	had been carrying
he/she/it	carried	was carrying	had carried	had been carrying
we	carried	were carrying	had carried	had been carrying
you	carried	were carrying	had carried	had been carrying
they	carried	were carrying	had carried	had been carrying

Future

	Future simple	Future continuous	Future perfect simple	Future perfect continuous
I	will carry	will be carrying	will have carried	will have been carrying
you	will carry	will be carrying	will have carried	will have been carrying
he/she/it	will carry	will be carrying	will have carried	will have been carrying
we	will carry	will be carrying	will have carried	will have been carrying
you	will carry	will be carrying	will have carried	will have been carrying
they	will carry	will be carrying	will have carried	will have been carrying

Conditional

	Conditional	Conditional past
I	would carry	would have carried
you	would carry	would have carried
he/she/it	would carry	would have carried
we	would carry	would have carried
you	would carry	would have carried
they	would carry	would have carried

Imperative
carry

Gerund
carrying

Past participle
carried

catch [kætʃ] *fangen*

Present

	Present simple	Present continuous	Present perfect simple	Present perfect continuous
I	catch	am catching	have caught	have been catching
you	catch	are catching	have caught	have been catching
he/she/it	catches	is catching	has caught	has been catching
we	catch	are catching	have caught	have been catching
you	catch	are catching	have caught	have been catching
they	catch	are catching	have caught	have been catching

Past

	Past simple	Past continuous	Past perfect simple	Past perfect continuous
I	caught	was catching	had caught	had been catching
you	caught	were catching	had caught	had been catching
he/she/it	caught	was catching	had caught	had been catching
we	caught	were catching	had caught	had been catching
you	caught	were catching	had caught	had been catching
they	caught	were catching	had caught	had been catching

Future

	Future simple	Future continuous	Future perfect simple	Future perfect continuous
I	will catch	will be catching	will have caught	will have been catching
you	will catch	will be catching	will have caught	will have been catching
he/she/it	will catch	will be catching	will have caught	will have been catching
we	will catch	will be catching	will have caught	will have been catching
you	will catch	will be catching	will have caught	will have been catching
they	will catch	will be catching	will have caught	will have been catching

Conditional

	Conditional	Conditional past
I	would catch	would have caught
you	would catch	would have caught
he/she/it	would catch	would have caught
we	would catch	would have caught
you	would catch	would have caught
they	would catch	would have caught

Imperative
catch

Gerund
catching

Past participle
caught

check [tʃek] *(nach)prüfen*

Present

	Present simple	Present continuous	Present perfect simple	Present perfect continuous
I	check	am checking	have checked	have been checking
you	check	are checking	have checked	have been checking
he/she/it	checks	is checking	has checked	has been checking
we	check	are checking	have checked	have been checking
you	check	are checking	have checked	have been checking
they	check	are checking	have checked	have been checking

Past

	Past simple	Past continuous	Past perfect simple	Past perfect continuous
I	checked	was checking	had checked	had been checking
you	checked	were checking	had checked	had been checking
he/she/it	checked	was checking	had checked	had been checking
we	checked	were checking	had checked	had been checking
you	checked	were checking	had checked	had been checking
they	checked	were checking	had checked	had been checking

Future

	Future simple	Future continuous	Future perfect simple	Future perfect continuous
I	will check	will be checking	will have checked	will have been checking
you	will check	will be checking	will have checked	will have been checking
he/she/it	will check	will be checking	will have checked	will have been checking
we	will check	will be checking	will have checked	will have been checking
you	will check	will be checking	will have checked	will have been checking
they	will check	will be checking	will have checked	will have been checking

Conditional

	Conditional	Conditional past
I	would check	would have checked
you	would check	would have checked
he/she/it	would check	would have checked
we	would check	would have checked
you	would check	would have checked
they	would check	would have checked

Imperative
check

Gerund
checking

Past participle
checked

choose [tʃu:z] *(aus)wählen*

Present

	Present simple	Present continuous	Present perfect simple	Present perfect continuous
I	choose	am choosing	have chosen	have been choosing
you	choose	are choosing	have chosen	have been choosing
he/she/it	chooses	is choosing	has chosen	has been choosing
we	choose	are choosing	have chosen	have been choosing
you	choose	are choosing	have chosen	have been choosing
they	choose	are choosing	have chosen	have been choosing

Past

	Past simple	Past continuous	Past perfect simple	Past perfect continuous
I	chose	was choosing	had chosen	had been choosing
you	chose	were choosing	had chosen	had been choosing
he/she/it	chose	was choosing	had chosen	had been choosing
we	chose	were choosing	had chosen	had been choosing
you	chose	were choosing	had chosen	had been choosing
they	chose	were choosing	had chosen	had been choosing

Future

	Future simple	Future continuous	Future perfect simple	Future perfect continuous
I	will choose	will be choosing	will have chosen	will have been choosing
you	will choose	will be choosing	will have chosen	will have been choosing
he/she/it	will choose	will be choosing	will have chosen	will have been choosing
we	will choose	will be choosing	will have chosen	will have been choosing
you	will choose	will be choosing	will have chosen	will have been choosing
they	will choose	will be choosing	will have chosen	will have been choosing

Conditional

	Conditional	Conditional past
I	would choose	would have chosen
you	would choose	would have chosen
he/she/it	would choose	would have chosen
we	would choose	would have chosen
you	would choose	would have chosen
they	would choose	would have chosen

Imperative
choose

Gerund
choosing

Past participle
chosen

come [kʌm] *kommen*

Present

	Present simple	Present continuous	Present perfect simple	Present perfect continuous
I	come	am coming	have come	have been coming
you	come	are coming	have come	have been coming
he/she/it	comes	is coming	has come	has been coming
we	come	are coming	have come	have been coming
you	come	are coming	have come	have been coming
they	come	are coming	have come	have been coming

Past

	Past simple	Past continuous	Past perfect simple	Past perfect continuous
I	came	was coming	had come	had been coming
you	came	were coming	had come	had been coming
he/she/it	came	was coming	had come	had been coming
we	came	were coming	had come	had been coming
you	came	were coming	had come	had been coming
they	came	were coming	had come	had been coming

Future

	Future simple	Future continuous	Future perfect simple	Future perfect continuous
I	will come	will be coming	will have come	will have been coming
you	will come	will be coming	will have come	will have been coming
he/she/it	will come	will be coming	will have come	will have been coming
we	will come	will be coming	will have come	will have been coming
you	will come	will be coming	will have come	will have been coming
they	will come	will be coming	will have come	will have been coming

Conditional

	Conditional	Conditional past
I	would come	would have come
you	would come	would have come
he/she/it	would come	would have come
we	would come	would have come
you	would come	would have come
they	would come	would have come

Imperative
come

Gerund
coming

Past participle
come

cost [kɔst] *kosten*

Present

	Present simple	Present continuous	Present perfect simple	Present perfect continuous
I	cost	am costing	have cost	have been costing
you	cost	are costing	have cost	have been costing
he/she/it	costs	is costing	has cost	has been costing
we	cost	are costing	have cost	have been costing
you	cost	are costing	have cost	have been costing
they	cost	are costing	have cost	have been costing

Past

	Past simple	Past continuous	Past perfect simple	Past perfect continuous
I	cost	was costing	had cost	had been costing
you	cost	were costing	had cost	had been costing
he/she/it	cost	was costing	had cost	had been costing
we	cost	were costing	had cost	had been costing
you	cost	were costing	had cost	had been costing
they	cost	were costing	had cost	had been costing

Future

	Future simple	Future continuous	Future perfect simple	Future perfect continuous
I	will cost	will be costing	will have cost	will have been costing
you	will cost	will be costing	will have cost	will have been costing
he/she/it	will cost	will be costing	will have cost	will have been costing
we	will cost	will be costing	will have cost	will have been costing
you	will cost	will be costing	will have cost	will have been costing
they	will cost	will be costing	will have cost	will have been costing

Conditional

	Conditional	Conditional past
I	would cost	would have cost
you	would cost	would have cost
he/she/it	would cost	would have cost
we	would cost	would have cost
you	would cost	would have cost
they	would cost	would have cost

Imperative
cost

Gerund
costing

Past participle
cost

cut [kʌt] *schneiden*

Present

	Present simple	Present continuous	Present perfect simple	Present perfect continuous
I	cut	am cutting	have cut	have been cutting
you	cut	are cutting	have cut	have been cutting
he/she/it	cuts	is cutting	has cut	has been cutting
we	cut	are cutting	have cut	have been cutting
you	cut	are cutting	have cut	have been cutting
they	cut	are cutting	have cut	have been cutting

Past

	Past simple	Past continuous	Past perfect simple	Past perfect continuous
I	cut	was cutting	had cut	had been cutting
you	cut	were cutting	had cut	had been cutting
he/she/it	cut	was cutting	had cut	had been cutting
we	cut	were cutting	had cut	had been cutting
you	cut	were cutting	had cut	had been cutting
they	cut	were cutting	had cut	had been cutting

Future

	Future simple	Future continuous	Future perfect simple	Future perfect continuous
I	will cut	will be cutting	will have cut	will have been cutting
you	will cut	will be cutting	will have cut	will have been cutting
he/she/it	will cut	will be cutting	will have cut	will have been cutting
we	will cut	will be cutting	will have cut	will have been cutting
you	will cut	will be cutting	will have cut	will have been cutting
they	will cut	will be cutting	will have cut	will have been cutting

Conditional

	Conditional	Conditional past
I	would cut	would have cut
you	would cut	would have cut
he/she/it	would cut	would have cut
we	would cut	would have cut
you	would cut	would have cut
they	would cut	would have cut

Imperative
cut

Gerund
cutting

Past participle
cut

decide [dɪ'saɪd] *(sich) entscheiden*

Present

	Present simple	Present continuous	Present perfect simple	Present perfect continuous
I	decide	am deciding	have decided	have been deciding
you	decide	are deciding	have decided	have been deciding
he/she/it	decides	is deciding	has decided	has been deciding
we	decide	are deciding	have decided	have been deciding
you	decide	are deciding	have decided	have been deciding
they	decide	are deciding	have decided	have been deciding

Past

	Past simple	Past continuous	Past perfect simple	Past perfect continuous
I	decided	was deciding	had decided	had been deciding
you	decided	were deciding	had decided	had been deciding
he/she/it	decided	was deciding	had decided	had been deciding
we	decided	were deciding	had decided	had been deciding
you	decided	were deciding	had decided	had been deciding
they	decided	were deciding	had decided	had been deciding

Future

	Future simple	Future continuous	Future perfect simple	Future perfect continuous
I	will decide	will be deciding	will have decided	will have been deciding
you	will decide	will be deciding	will have decided	will have been deciding
he/she/it	will decide	will be deciding	will have decided	will have been deciding
we	will decide	will be deciding	will have decided	will have been deciding
you	will decide	will be deciding	will have decided	will have been deciding
they	will decide	will be deciding	will have decided	will have been deciding

Conditional

	Conditional	Conditional past
I	would decide	would have decided
you	would decide	would have decided
he/she/it	would decide	would have decided
we	would decide	would have decided
you	would decide	would have decided
they	would decide	would have decided

Imperative
decide

Gerund
deciding

Past participle
decided

do [du:] *tun, machen*

Present

	Present simple	Present continuous	Present perfect simple	Present perfect continuous
I	do	am doing	have **done**	have been doing
you	do	are doing	have **done**	have been doing
he/she/it	do**es**	is doing	has **done**	has been doing
we	do	are doing	have **done**	have been doing
you	do	are doing	have **done**	have been doing
they	do	are doing	have **done**	have been doing

Past

	Past simple	Past continuous	Past perfect simple	Past perfect continuous
I	**did**	was doing	had **done**	had been doing
you	**did**	were doing	had **done**	had been doing
he/she/it	**did**	was doing	had **done**	had been doing
we	**did**	were doing	had **done**	had been doing
you	**did**	were doing	had **done**	had been doing
they	**did**	were doing	had **done**	had been doing

Future

	Future simple	Future continuous	Future perfect simple	Future perfect continuous
I	will do	will be doing	will have **done**	will have been doing
you	will do	will be doing	will have **done**	will have been doing
he/she/it	will do	will be doing	will have **done**	will have been doing
we	will do	will be doing	will have **done**	will have been doing
you	will do	will be doing	will have **done**	will have been doing
they	will do	will be doing	will have **done**	will have been doing

Conditional

	Conditional	Conditional past
I	would do	would have **done**
you	would do	would have **done**
he/she/it	would do	would have **done**
we	would do	would have **done**
you	would do	would have **done**
they	would do	would have **done**

Imperative
do

Gerund
doing

Past participle
done

drink [drɪŋk] *trinken*

Present

	Present simple	Present continuous	Present perfect simple	Present perfect continuous
I	drink	am drinking	have **drunk**	have been drinking
you	drink	are drinking	have **drunk**	have been drinking
he/she/it	drink**s**	is drinking	has **drunk**	has been drinking
we	drink	are drinking	have **drunk**	have been drinking
you	drink	are drinking	have **drunk**	have been drinking
they	drink	are drinking	have **drunk**	have been drinking

Past

	Past simple	Past continuous	Past perfect simple	Past perfect continuous
I	**drank**	was drinking	had **drunk**	had been drinking
you	**drank**	were drinking	had **drunk**	had been drinking
he/she/it	**drank**	was drinking	had **drunk**	had been drinking
we	**drank**	were drinking	had **drunk**	had been drinking
you	**drank**	were drinking	had **drunk**	had been drinking
they	**drank**	were drinking	had **drunk**	had been drinking

Future

	Future simple	Future continuous	Future perfect simple	Future perfect continuous
I	will drink	will be drinking	will have **drunk**	will have been drinking
you	will drink	will be drinking	will have **drunk**	will have been drinking
he/she/it	will drink	will be drinking	will have **drunk**	will have been drinking
we	will drink	will be drinking	will have **drunk**	will have been drinking
you	will drink	will be drinking	will have **drunk**	will have been drinking
they	will drink	will be drinking	will have **drunk**	will have been drinking

Conditional

	Conditional	Conditional past
I	would drink	would have **drunk**
you	would drink	would have **drunk**
he/she/it	would drink	would have **drunk**
we	would drink	would have **drunk**
you	would drink	would have **drunk**
they	would drink	would have **drunk**

Imperative
drink

Gerund
drinking

Past participle
drunk

drive [draɪv] *fahren*

Present

	Present simple	Present continuous	Present perfect simple	Present perfect continuous
I	drive	am driving	have driven	have been driving
you	drive	are driving	have driven	have been driving
he/she/it	drives	is driving	has driven	has been driving
we	drive	are driving	have driven	have been driving
you	drive	are driving	have driven	have been driving
they	drive	are driving	have driven	have been driving

Past

	Past simple	Past continuous	Past perfect simple	Past perfect continuous
I	drove	was driving	had driven	had been driving
you	drove	were driving	had driven	had been driving
he/she/it	drove	was driving	had driven	had been driving
we	drove	were driving	had driven	had been driving
you	drove	were driving	had driven	had been driving
they	drove	were driving	had driven	had been driving

Future

	Future simple	Future continuous	Future perfect simple	Future perfect continuous
I	will drive	will be driving	will have driven	will have been driving
you	will drive	will be driving	will have driven	will have been driving
he/she/it	will drive	will be driving	will have driven	will have been driving
we	will drive	will be driving	will have driven	will have been driving
you	will drive	will be driving	will have driven	will have been driving
they	will drive	will be driving	will have driven	will have been driving

Conditional

	Conditional	Conditional past
I	would drive	would have driven
you	would drive	would have driven
he/she/it	would drive	would have driven
we	would drive	would have driven
you	would drive	would have driven
they	would drive	would have driven

Imperative
drive

Gerund
driving

Past participle
driven

eat [i:t] *essen*

Present

	Present simple	Present continuous	Present perfect simple	Present perfect continuous
I	eat	am eating	have eaten	have been eating
you	eat	are eating	have eaten	have been eating
he/she/it	eats	is eating	has eaten	has been eating
we	eat	are eating	have eaten	have been eating
you	eat	are eating	have eaten	have been eating
they	eat	are eating	have eaten	have been eating

Past

	Past simple	Past continuous	Past perfect simple	Past perfect continuous
I	ate	was eating	had eaten	had been eating
you	ate	were eating	had eaten	had been eating
he/she/it	ate	was eating	had eaten	had been eating
we	ate	were eating	had eaten	had been eating
you	ate	were eating	had eaten	had been eating
they	ate	were eating	had eaten	had been eating

Future

	Future simple	Future continuous	Future perfect simple	Future perfect continuous
I	will eat	will be eating	will have eaten	will have been eating
you	will eat	will be eating	will have eaten	will have been eating
he/she/it	will eat	will be eating	will have eaten	will have been eating
we	will eat	will be eating	will have eaten	will have been eating
you	will eat	will be eating	will have eaten	will have been eating
they	will eat	will be eating	will have eaten	will have been eating

Conditional

	Conditional	Conditional past
I	would eat	would have eaten
you	would eat	would have eaten
he/she/it	would eat	would have eaten
we	would eat	would have eaten
you	would eat	would have eaten
they	would eat	would have eaten

Imperative
eat

Gerund
eating

Past participle
eaten

enjoy [ɪn'dʒɔɪ] *genießen*

Present

	Present simple	Present continuous	Present perfect simple	Present perfect continuous
I	enjoy	am enjoying	have enjoyed	have been enjoying
you	enjoy	are enjoying	have enjoyed	have been enjoying
he/she/it	enjoys	is enjoying	has enjoyed	has been enjoying
we	enjoy	are enjoying	have enjoyed	have been enjoying
you	enjoy	are enjoying	have enjoyed	have been enjoying
they	enjoy	are enjoying	have enjoyed	have been enjoying

Past

	Past simple	Past continuous	Past perfect simple	Past perfect continuous
I	enjoyed	was enjoying	had enjoyed	had been enjoying
you	enjoyed	were enjoying	had enjoyed	had been enjoying
he/she/it	enjoyed	was enjoying	had enjoyed	had been enjoying
we	enjoyed	were enjoying	had enjoyed	had been enjoying
you	enjoyed	were enjoying	had enjoyed	had been enjoying
they	enjoyed	were enjoying	had enjoyed	had been enjoying

Future

	Future simple	Future continuous	Future perfect simple	Future perfect continuous
I	will enjoy	will be enjoying	will have enjoyed	will have been enjoying
you	will enjoy	will be enjoying	will have enjoyed	will have been enjoying
he/she/it	will enjoy	will be enjoying	will have enjoyed	will have been enjoying
we	will enjoy	will be enjoying	will have enjoyed	will have been enjoying
you	will enjoy	will be enjoying	will have enjoyed	will have been enjoying
they	will enjoy	will be enjoying	will have enjoyed	will have been enjoying

Conditional

	Conditional	Conditional past
I	would enjoy	would have enjoyed
you	would enjoy	would have enjoyed
he/she/it	would enjoy	would have enjoyed
we	would enjoy	would have enjoyed
you	would enjoy	would have enjoyed
they	would enjoy	would have enjoyed

Imperative
enjoy

Gerund
enjoying

Past participle
enjoyed

fall [fɔ:l] *fallen*

Present

	Present simple	Present continuous	Present perfect simple	Present perfect continuous
I	fall	am falling	have **fallen**	have been falling
you	fall	are falling	have **fallen**	have been falling
he/she/it	fall**s**	is falling	has **fallen**	has been falling
we	fall	are falling	have **fallen**	have been falling
you	fall	are falling	have **fallen**	have been falling
they	fall	are falling	have **fallen**	have been falling

Past

	Past simple	Past continuous	Past perfect simple	Past perfect continuous
I	**fell**	was falling	had **fallen**	had been falling
you	**fell**	were falling	had **fallen**	had been falling
he/she/it	**fell**	was falling	had **fallen**	had been falling
we	**fell**	were falling	had **fallen**	had been falling
you	**fell**	were falling	had **fallen**	had been falling
they	**fell**	were falling	had **fallen**	had been falling

Future

	Future simple	Future continuous	Future perfect simple	Future perfect continuous
I	will fall	will be falling	will have **fallen**	will have been falling
you	will fall	will be falling	will have **fallen**	will have been falling
he/she/it	will fall	will be falling	will have **fallen**	will have been falling
we	will fall	will be falling	will have **fallen**	will have been falling
you	will fall	will be falling	will have **fallen**	will have been falling
they	will fall	will be falling	will have **fallen**	will have been falling

Conditional

	Conditional	Conditional past
I	would fall	would have **fallen**
you	would fall	would have **fallen**
he/she/it	would fall	would have **fallen**
we	would fall	would have **fallen**
you	would fall	would have **fallen**
they	would fall	would have **fallen**

Imperative
fall

Gerund
falling

Past participle
fallen

feel [fi:l] *fühlen*

Present

	Present simple	Present continuous	Present perfect simple	Present perfect continuous
I	feel	am feeling	have felt	have been feeling
you	feel	are feeling	have felt	have been feeling
he/she/it	feels	is feeling	has felt	has been feeling
we	feel	are feeling	have felt	have been feeling
you	feel	are feeling	have felt	have been feeling
they	feel	are feeling	have felt	have been feeling

Past

	Past simple	Past continuous	Past perfect simple	Past perfect continuous
I	felt	was feeling	had felt	had been feeling
you	felt	were feeling	had felt	had been feeling
he/she/it	felt	was feeling	had felt	had been feeling
we	felt	were feeling	had felt	had been feeling
you	felt	were feeling	had felt	had been feeling
they	felt	were feeling	had felt	had been feeling

Future

	Future simple	Future continuous	Future perfect simple	Future perfect continuous
I	will feel	will be feeling	will have felt	will have been feeling
you	will feel	will be feeling	will have felt	will have been feeling
he/she/it	will feel	will be feeling	will have felt	will have been feeling
we	will feel	will be feeling	will have felt	will have been feeling
you	will feel	will be feeling	will have felt	will have been feeling
they	will feel	will be feeling	will have felt	will have been feeling

Conditional

	Conditional	Conditional past
I	would feel	would have felt
you	would feel	would have felt
he/she/it	would feel	would have felt
we	would feel	would have felt
you	would feel	would have felt
they	would feel	would have felt

Imperative
feel

Gerund
feeling

Past participle
felt

fight [faɪt] *kämpfen*

Present

	Present simple	Present continuous	Present perfect simple	Present perfect continuous
I	fight	am fighting	have fought	have been fighting
you	fight	are fighting	have fought	have been fighting
he/she/it	fights	is fighting	has fought	has been fighting
we	fight	are fighting	have fought	have been fighting
you	fight	are fighting	have fought	have been fighting
they	fight	are fighting	have fought	have been fighting

Past

	Past simple	Past continuous	Past perfect simple	Past perfect continuous
I	fought	was fighting	had fought	had been fighting
you	fought	were fighting	had fought	had been fighting
he/she/it	fought	was fighting	had fought	had been fighting
we	fought	were fighting	had fought	had been fighting
you	fought	were fighting	had fought	had been fighting
they	fought	were fighting	had fought	had been fighting

Future

	Future simple	Future continuous	Future perfect simple	Future perfect continuous
I	will fight	will be fighting	will have fought	will have been fighting
you	will fight	will be fighting	will have fought	will have been fighting
he/she/it	will fight	will be fighting	will have fought	will have been fighting
we	will fight	will be fighting	will have fought	will have been fighting
you	will fight	will be fighting	will have fought	will have been fighting
they	will fight	will be fighting	will have fought	will have been fighting

Conditional

	Conditional	Conditional past
I	would fight	would have fought
you	would fight	would have fought
he/she/it	would fight	would have fought
we	would fight	would have fought
you	would fight	would have fought
they	would fight	would have fought

Imperative
fight

Gerund
fighting

Past participle
fought

find [faɪnd] *finden*

Present

	Present simple	Present continuous	Present perfect simple	Present perfect continuous
I	find	am finding	have found	have been finding
you	find	are finding	have found	have been finding
he/she/it	finds	is finding	has found	has been finding
we	find	are finding	have found	have been finding
you	find	are finding	have found	have been finding
they	find	are finding	have found	have been finding

Past

	Past simple	Past continuous	Past perfect simple	Past perfect continuous
I	found	was finding	had found	had been finding
you	found	were finding	had found	had been finding
he/she/it	found	was finding	had found	had been finding
we	found	were finding	had found	had been finding
you	found	were finding	had found	had been finding
they	found	were finding	had found	had been finding

Future

	Future simple	Future continuous	Future perfect simple	Future perfect continuous
I	will find	will be finding	will have found	will have been finding
you	will find	will be finding	will have found	will have been finding
he/she/it	will find	will be finding	will have found	will have been finding
we	will find	will be finding	will have found	will have been finding
you	will find	will be finding	will have found	will have been finding
they	will find	will be finding	will have found	will have been finding

Conditional

	Conditional	Conditional past
I	would find	would have found
you	would find	would have found
he/she/it	would find	would have found
we	would find	would have found
you	would find	would have found
they	would find	would have found

Imperative
find

Gerund
finding

Past participle
found

fly [flaɪ] *fliegen*

Present

	Present simple	Present continuous	Present perfect simple	Present perfect continuous
I	fly	am flying	have **flown**	have been flying
you	fly	are flying	have **flown**	have been flying
he/she/it	fl**ies**	is flying	has **flown**	has been flying
we	fly	are flying	have **flown**	have been flying
you	fly	are flying	have **flown**	have been flying
they	fly	are flying	have **flown**	have been flying

Past

	Past simple	Past continuous	Past perfect simple	Past perfect continuous
I	**flew**	was flying	had **flown**	had been flying
you	**flew**	were flying	had **flown**	had been flying
he/she/it	**flew**	was flying	had **flown**	had been flying
we	**flew**	were flying	had **flown**	had been flying
you	**flew**	were flying	had **flown**	had been flying
they	**flew**	were flying	had **flown**	had been flying

Future

	Future simple	Future continuous	Future perfect simple	Future perfect continuous
I	will fly	will be flying	will have **flown**	will have been flying
you	will fly	will be flying	will have **flown**	will have been flying
he/she/it	will fly	will be flying	will have **flown**	will have been flying
we	will fly	will be flying	will have **flown**	will have been flying
you	will fly	will be flying	will have **flown**	will have been flying
they	will fly	will be flying	will have **flown**	will have been flying

Conditional

	Conditional	Conditional past
I	would fly	would have **flown**
you	would fly	would have **flown**
he/she/it	would fly	would have **flown**
we	would fly	would have **flown**
you	would fly	would have **flown**
they	would fly	would have **flown**

Imperative
fly

Gerund
flying

Past participle
flown

forget [fə'get] *vergessen*

Present

	Present simple	Present continuous	Present perfect simple	Present perfect continuous
I	forget	am forgetting	have forgotten	have been forgetting
you	forget	are forgetting	have forgotten	have been forgetting
he/she/it	forgets	is forgetting	has forgotten	has been forgetting
we	forget	are forgetting	have forgotten	have been forgetting
you	forget	are forgetting	have forgotten	have been forgetting
they	forget	are forgetting	have forgotten	have been forgetting

Past

	Past simple	Past continuous	Past perfect simple	Past perfect continuous
I	forgot	was forgetting	had forgotten	had been forgetting
you	forgot	were forgetting	had forgotten	had been forgetting
he/she/it	forgot	was forgetting	had forgotten	had been forgetting
we	forgot	were forgetting	had forgotten	had been forgetting
you	forgot	were forgetting	had forgotten	had been forgetting
they	forgot	were forgetting	had forgotten	had been forgetting

Future

	Future simple	Future continuous	Future perfect simple	Future perfect continuous
I	will forget	will be forgetting	will have forgotten	will have been forgetting
you	will forget	will be forgetting	will have forgotten	will have been forgetting
he/she/it	will forget	will be forgetting	will have forgotten	will have been forgetting
we	will forget	will be forgetting	will have forgotten	will have been forgetting
you	will forget	will be forgetting	will have forgotten	will have been forgetting
they	will forget	will be forgetting	will have forgotten	will have been forgetting

Conditional

	Conditional	Conditional past
I	would forget	would have forgotten
you	would forget	would have forgotten
he/she/it	would forget	would have forgotten
we	would forget	would have forgotten
you	would forget	would have forgotten
they	would forget	would have forgotten

Imperative
forget

Gerund
forgetting

Past participle
forgotten

get [get] *bekommen*

Present

	Present simple	Present continuous	Present perfect simple	Present perfect continuous
I	get	am getting	have got	have been getting
you	get	are getting	have got	have been getting
he/she/it	gets	is getting	has got	has been getting
we	get	are getting	have got	have been getting
you	get	are getting	have got	have been getting
they	get	are getting	have got	have been getting

Past

	Past simple	Past continuous	Past perfect simple	Past perfect continuous
I	got	was getting	had got	had been getting
you	got	were getting	had got	had been getting
he/she/it	got	was getting	had got	had been getting
we	got	were getting	had got	had been getting
you	got	were getting	had got	had been getting
they	got	were getting	had got	had been getting

Future

	Future simple	Future continuous	Future perfect simple	Future perfect continuous
I	will get	will be getting	will have got	will have been getting
you	will get	will be getting	will have got	will have been getting
he/she/it	will get	will be getting	will have got	will have been getting
we	will get	will be getting	will have got	will have been getting
you	will get	will be getting	will have got	will have been getting
they	will get	will be getting	will have got	will have been getting

Conditional

	Conditional	Conditional past
I	would get	would have got
you	would get	would have got
he/she/it	would get	would have got
we	would get	would have got
you	would get	would have got
they	would get	would have got

Imperative
get

Gerund
getting

Past participle
got / gotten (AE)

give [gɪv] *geben*

Present

	Present simple	Present continuous	Present perfect simple	Present perfect continuous
I	give	am giving	have given	have been giving
you	give	are giving	have given	have been giving
he/she/it	gives	is giving	has given	has been giving
we	give	are giving	have given	have been giving
you	give	are giving	have given	have been giving
they	give	are giving	have given	have been giving

Past

	Past simple	Past continuous	Past perfect simple	Past perfect continuous
I	gave	was giving	had given	had been giving
you	gave	were giving	had given	had been giving
he/she/it	gave	was giving	had given	had been giving
we	gave	were giving	had given	had been giving
you	gave	were giving	had given	had been giving
they	gave	were giving	had given	had been giving

Future

	Future simple	Future continuous	Future perfect simple	Future perfect continuous
I	will give	will be giving	will have given	will have been giving
you	will give	will be giving	will have given	will have been giving
he/she/it	will give	will be giving	will have given	will have been giving
we	will give	will be giving	will have given	will have been giving
you	will give	will be giving	will have given	will have been giving
they	will give	will be giving	will have given	will have been giving

Conditional

	Conditional	Conditional past
I	would give	would have given
you	would give	would have given
he/she/it	would give	would have given
we	would give	would have given
you	would give	would have given
they	would give	would have given

Imperative
give

Gerund
giving

Past participle
given

go [gəʊ] *gehen*

Present

	Present simple	Present continuous	Present perfect simple	Present perfect continuous
I	go	am going	have gone	have been going
you	go	are going	have gone	have been going
he/she/it	goes	is going	has gone	has been going
we	go	are going	have gone	have been going
you	go	are going	have gone	have been going
they	go	are going	have gone	have been going

Past

	Past simple	Past continuous	Past perfect simple	Past perfect continuous
I	went	was going	had gone	had been going
you	went	were going	had gone	had been going
he/she/it	went	was going	had gone	had been going
we	went	were going	had gone	had been going
you	went	were going	had gone	had been going
they	went	were going	had gone	had been going

Future

	Future simple	Future continuous	Future perfect simple	Future perfect continuous
I	will go	will be going	will have gone	will have been going
you	will go	will be going	will have gone	will have been going
he/she/it	will go	will be going	will have gone	will have been going
we	will go	will be going	will have gone	will have been going
you	will go	will be going	will have gone	will have been going
they	will go	will be going	will have gone	will have been going

Conditional

	Conditional	Conditional past
I	would go	would have gone
you	would go	would have gone
he/she/it	would go	would have gone
we	would go	would have gone
you	would go	would have gone
they	would go	would have gone

Imperative
go

Gerund
going

Past participle
gone

have [hæv] *haben*

Present

	Present simple	Present continuous	Present perfect simple	Present perfect continuous
I	have	am having	have had	have been having
you	have	are having	have had	have been having
he/she/it	has	is having	has had	has been having
we	have	are having	have had	have been having
you	have	are having	have had	have been having
they	have	are having	have had	have been having

Past

	Past simple	Past continuous	Past perfect simple	Past perfect continuous
I	had	was having	had had	had been having
you	had	were having	had had	had been having
he/she/it	had	was having	had had	had been having
we	had	were having	had had	had been having
you	had	were having	had had	had been having
they	had	were having	had had	had been having

Future

	Future simple	Future continuous	Future perfect simple	Future perfect continuous
I	will have	will be having	will have had	will have been having
you	will have	will be having	will have had	will have been having
he/she/it	will have	will be having	will have had	will have been having
we	will have	will be having	will have had	will have been having
you	will have	will be having	will have had	will have been having
they	will have	will be having	will have had	will have been having

Conditional

	Conditional	Conditional past
I	would have	would have had
you	would have	would have had
he/she/it	would have	would have had
we	would have	would have had
you	would have	would have had
they	would have	would have had

Imperative
have

Gerund
having

Past participle
had

hear [hɪə] *hören*

Present

	Present simple	Present continuous	Present perfect simple	Present perfect continuous
I	hear	am hearing	have heard	have been hearing
you	hear	are hearing	have heard	have been hearing
he/she/it	hears	is hearing	has heard	has been hearing
we	hear	are hearing	have heard	have been hearing
you	hear	are hearing	have heard	have been hearing
they	hear	are hearing	have heard	have been hearing

Past

	Past simple	Past continuous	Past perfect simple	Past perfect continuous
I	heard	was hearing	had heard	had been hearing
you	heard	were hearing	had heard	had been hearing
he/she/it	heard	was hearing	had heard	had been hearing
we	heard	were hearing	had heard	had been hearing
you	heard	were hearing	had heard	had been hearing
they	heard	were hearing	had heard	had been hearing

Future

	Future simple	Future continuous	Future perfect simple	Future perfect continuous
I	will hear	will be hearing	will have heard	will have been hearing
you	will hear	will be hearing	will have heard	will have been hearing
he/she/it	will hear	will be hearing	will have heard	will have been hearing
we	will hear	will be hearing	will have heard	will have been hearing
you	will hear	will be hearing	will have heard	will have been hearing
they	will hear	will be hearing	will have heard	will have been hearing

Conditional

	Conditional	Conditional past
I	would hear	would have heard
you	would hear	would have heard
he/she/it	would hear	would have heard
we	would hear	would have heard
you	would hear	would have heard
they	would hear	would have heard

Imperative
hear

Gerund
hearing

Past participle
heard

help [help] *helfen*

Present

	Present simple	Present continuous	Present perfect simple	Present perfect continuous
I	help	am helping	have helped	have been helping
you	help	are helping	have helped	have been helping
he/she/it	helps	is helping	has helped	has been helping
we	help	are helping	have helped	have been helping
you	help	are helping	have helped	have been helping
they	help	are helping	have helped	have been helping

Past

	Past simple	Past continuous	Past perfect simple	Past perfect continuous
I	helped	was helping	had helped	had been helping
you	helped	were helping	had helped	had been helping
he/she/it	helped	was helping	had helped	had been helping
we	helped	were helping	had helped	had been helping
you	helped	were helping	had helped	had been helping
they	helped	were helping	had helped	had been helping

Future

	Future simple	Future continuous	Future perfect simple	Future perfect continuous
I	will help	will be helping	will have helped	will have been helping
you	will help	will be helping	will have helped	will have been helping
he/she/it	will help	will be helping	will have helped	will have been helping
we	will help	will be helping	will have helped	will have been helping
you	will help	will be helping	will have helped	will have been helping
they	will help	will be helping	will have helped	will have been helping

Conditional

	Conditional	Conditional past
I	would help	would have helped
you	would help	would have helped
he/she/it	would help	would have helped
we	would help	would have helped
you	would help	would have helped
they	would help	would have helped

Imperative
help

Gerund
helping

Past participle
helped

hire ['haɪə] *(ver)mieten, einstellen (AE)*

Present

	Present simple	Present continuous	Present perfect simple	Present perfect continuous
I	hire	am hiring	have hired	have been hiring
you	hire	are hiring	have hired	have been hiring
he/she/it	hires	is hiring	has hired	has been hiring
we	hire	are hiring	have hired	have been hiring
you	hire	are hiring	have hired	have been hiring
they	hire	are hiring	have hired	have been hiring

Past

	Past simple	Past continuous	Past perfect simple	Past perfect continuous
I	hired	was hiring	had hired	had been hiring
you	hired	were hiring	had hired	had been hiring
he/she/it	hired	was hiring	had hired	had been hiring
we	hired	were hiring	had hired	had been hiring
you	hired	were hiring	had hired	had been hiring
they	hired	were hiring	had hired	had been hiring

Future

	Future simple	Future continuous	Future perfect simple	Future perfect continuous
I	will hire	will be hiring	will have hired	will have been hiring
you	will hire	will be hiring	will have hired	will have been hiring
he/she/it	will hire	will be hiring	will have hired	will have been hiring
we	will hire	will be hiring	will have hired	will have been hiring
you	will hire	will be hiring	will have hired	will have been hiring
they	will hire	will be hiring	will have hired	will have been hiring

Conditional

	Conditional	Conditional past
I	would hire	would have hired
you	would hire	would have hired
he/she/it	would hire	would have hired
we	would hire	would have hired
you	would hire	would have hired
they	would hire	would have hired

Imperative
hire

Gerund
hiring

Past participle
hired

hurt [hɜːt] *weh tun, verletzen*

Present

	Present simple	Present continuous	Present perfect simple	Present perfect continuous
I	hurt	am hurting	have hurt	have been hurting
you	hurt	are hurting	have hurt	have been hurting
he/she/it	hurts	is hurting	has hurt	has been hurting
we	hurt	are hurting	have hurt	have been hurting
you	hurt	are hurting	have hurt	have been hurting
they	hurt	are hurting	have hurt	have been hurting

Past

	Past simple	Past continuous	Past perfect simple	Past perfect continuous
I	hurt	was hurting	had hurt	had been hurting
you	hurt	were hurting	had hurt	had been hurting
he/she/it	hurt	was hurting	had hurt	had been hurting
we	hurt	were hurting	had hurt	had been hurting
you	hurt	were hurting	had hurt	had been hurting
they	hurt	were hurting	had hurt	had been hurting

Future

	Future simple	Future continuous	Future perfect simple	Future perfect continuous
I	will hurt	will be hurting	will have hurt	will have been hurting
you	will hurt	will be hurting	will have hurt	will have been hurting
he/she/it	will hurt	will be hurting	will have hurt	will have been hurting
we	will hurt	will be hurting	will have hurt	will have been hurting
you	will hurt	will be hurting	will have hurt	will have been hurting
they	will hurt	will be hurting	will have hurt	will have been hurting

Conditional

	Conditional	Conditional past
I	would hurt	would have hurt
you	would hurt	would have hurt
he/she/it	would hurt	would have hurt
we	would hurt	would have hurt
you	would hurt	would have hurt
they	would hurt	would have hurt

Imperative
hurt

Gerund
hurting

Past participle
hurt

invite [ɪn'vaɪt] *einladen*

Present

	Present simple	Present continuous	Present perfect simple	Present perfect continuous
I	invite	am inviting	have invited	have been inviting
you	invite	are inviting	have invited	have been inviting
he/she/it	invites	is inviting	has invited	has been inviting
we	invite	are inviting	have invited	have been inviting
you	invite	are inviting	have invited	have been inviting
they	invite	are inviting	have invited	have been inviting

Past

	Past simple	Past continuous	Past perfect simple	Past perfect continuous
I	invited	was inviting	had invited	had been inviting
you	invited	were inviting	had invited	had been inviting
he/she/it	invited	was inviting	had invited	had been inviting
we	invited	were inviting	had invited	had been inviting
you	invited	were inviting	had invited	had been inviting
they	invited	were inviting	had invited	had been inviting

Future

	Future simple	Future continuous	Future perfect simple	Future perfect continuous
I	will invite	will be inviting	will have invited	will have been inviting
you	will invite	will be inviting	will have invited	will have been inviting
he/she/it	will invite	will be inviting	will have invited	will have been inviting
we	will invite	will be inviting	will have invited	will have been inviting
you	will invite	will be inviting	will have invited	will have been inviting
they	will invite	will be inviting	will have invited	will have been inviting

Conditional

	Conditional	Conditional past
I	would invite	would have invited
you	would invite	would have invited
he/she/it	would invite	would have invited
we	would invite	would have invited
you	would invite	would have invited
they	would invite	would have invited

Imperative
invite

Gerund
inviting

Past participle
invited

keep [ki:p] *behalten*

Present

	Present simple	Present continuous	Present perfect simple	Present perfect continuous
I	keep	am keeping	have kept	have been keeping
you	keep	are keeping	have kept	have been keeping
he/she/it	keeps	is keeping	has kept	has been keeping
we	keep	are keeping	have kept	have been keeping
you	keep	are keeping	have kept	have been keeping
they	keep	are keeping	have kept	have been keeping

Past

	Past simple	Past continuous	Past perfect simple	Past perfect continuous
I	kept	was keeping	had kept	had been keeping
you	kept	were keeping	had kept	had been keeping
he/she/it	kept	was keeping	had kept	had been keeping
we	kept	were keeping	had kept	had been keeping
you	kept	were keeping	had kept	had been keeping
they	kept	were keeping	had kept	had been keeping

Future

	Future simple	Future continuous	Future perfect simple	Future perfect continuous
I	will keep	will be keeping	will have kept	will have been keeping
you	will keep	will be keeping	will have kept	will have been keeping
he/she/it	will keep	will be keeping	will have kept	will have been keeping
we	will keep	will be keeping	will have kept	will have been keeping
you	will keep	will be keeping	will have kept	will have been keeping
they	will keep	will be keeping	will have kept	will have been keeping

Conditional

	Conditional	Conditional past
I	would keep	would have kept
you	would keep	would have kept
he/she/it	would keep	would have kept
we	would keep	would have kept
you	would keep	would have kept
they	would keep	would have kept

Imperative
keep

Gerund
keeping

Past participle
kept

know [nəʊ] *wissen, kennen*

▶ Die **continuous**-Formen sind nicht gebräuchlich.

Present

	Present simple	Present continuous	Present perfect simple	Present perfect continuous
I	know		have known	
you	know		have known	
he/she/it	knows		has known	
we	know		have known	
you	know		have known	
they	know		have known	

Past

	Past simple	Past continuous	Past perfect simple	Past perfect continuous
I	knew		had known	
you	knew		had known	
he/she/it	knew		had known	
we	knew		had known	
you	knew		had known	
they	knew		had known	

Future

	Future simple	Future continuous	Future perfect simple	Future perfect continuous
I	will know		will have known	
you	will know		will have known	
he/she/it	will know		will have known	
we	will know		will have known	
you	will know		will have known	
they	will know		will have known	

Conditional

	Conditional	Conditional past
I	would know	would have known
you	would know	would have known
he/she/it	would know	would have known
we	would know	would have known
you	would know	would have known
they	would know	would have known

Imperative
know

Gerund
knowing

Past participle
known

learn [lɜːn] *lernen*

Present

	Present simple	Present continuous	Present perfect simple	Present perfect continuous
I	learn	am learning	have learnt	have been learning
you	learn	are learning	have learnt	have been learning
he/she/it	learns	is learning	has learnt	has been learning
we	learn	are learning	have learnt	have been learning
you	learn	are learning	have learnt	have been learning
they	learn	are learning	have learnt	have been learning

Past

	Past simple	Past continuous	Past perfect simple	Past perfect continuous
I	learnt	was learning	had learnt	had been learning
you	learnt	were learning	had learnt	had been learning
he/she/it	learnt	was learning	had learnt	had been learning
we	learnt	were learning	had learnt	had been learning
you	learnt	were learning	had learnt	had been learning
they	learnt	were learning	had learnt	had been learning

Future

	Future simple	Future continuous	Future perfect simple	Future perfect continuous
I	will learn	will be learning	will have learnt	will have been learning
you	will learn	will be learning	will have learnt	will have been learning
he/she/it	will learn	will be learning	will have learnt	will have been learning
we	will learn	will be learning	will have learnt	will have been learning
you	will learn	will be learning	will have learnt	will have been learning
they	will learn	will be learning	will have learnt	will have been learning

Conditional

	Conditional	Conditional past
I	would learn	would have learnt
you	would learn	would have learnt
he/she/it	would learn	would have learnt
we	would learn	would have learnt
you	would learn	would have learnt
they	would learn	would have learnt

Imperative
learn

Gerund
learning

Past participle
learnt / learned (AE)

leave [li:v] *verlassen*

Present

	Present simple	Present continuous	Present perfect simple	Present perfect continuous
I	leave	am leaving	have left	have been leaving
you	leave	are leaving	have left	have been leaving
he/she/it	leaves	is leaving	has left	has been leaving
we	leave	are leaving	have left	have been leaving
you	leave	are leaving	have left	have been leaving
they	leave	are leaving	have left	have been leaving

Past

	Past simple	Past continuous	Past perfect simple	Past perfect continuous
I	left	was leaving	had left	had been leaving
you	left	were leaving	had left	had been leaving
he/she/it	left	was leaving	had left	had been leaving
we	left	were leaving	had left	had been leaving
you	left	were leaving	had left	had been leaving
they	left	were leaving	had left	had been leaving

Future

	Future simple	Future continuous	Future perfect simple	Future perfect continuous
I	will leave	will be leaving	will have left	will have been leaving
you	will leave	will be leaving	will have left	will have been leaving
he/she/it	will leave	will be leaving	will have left	will have been leaving
we	will leave	will be leaving	will have left	will have been leaving
you	will leave	will be leaving	will have left	will have been leaving
they	will leave	will be leaving	will have left	will have been leaving

Conditional

	Conditional	Conditional past
I	would leave	would have left
you	would leave	would have left
he/she/it	would leave	would have left
we	would leave	would have left
you	would leave	would have left
they	would leave	would have left

Imperative
leave

Gerund
leaving

Past participle
left

lend [lend] *(aus)leihen*

Present

	Present simple	Present continuous	Present perfect simple	Present perfect continuous
I	lend	am lending	have lent	have been lending
you	lend	are lending	have lent	have been lending
he/she/it	lends	is lending	has lent	has been lending
we	lend	are lending	have lent	have been lending
you	lend	are lending	have lent	have been lending
they	lend	are lending	have lent	have been lending

Past

	Past simple	Past continuous	Past perfect simple	Past perfect continuous
I	lent	was lending	had lent	had been lending
you	lent	were lending	had lent	had been lending
he/she/it	lent	was lending	had lent	had been lending
we	lent	were lending	had lent	had been lending
you	lent	were lending	had lent	had been lending
they	lent	were lending	had lent	had been lending

Future

	Future simple	Future continuous	Future perfect simple	Future perfect continuous
I	will lend	will be lending	will have lent	will have been lending
you	will lend	will be lending	will have lent	will have been lending
he/she/it	will lend	will be lending	will have lent	will have been lending
we	will lend	will be lending	will have lent	will have been lending
you	will lend	will be lending	will have lent	will have been lending
they	will lend	will be lending	will have lent	will have been lending

Conditional

	Conditional	Conditional past
I	would lend	would have lent
you	would lend	would have lent
he/she/it	would lend	would have lent
we	would lend	would have lent
you	would lend	would have lent
they	would lend	would have lent

Imperative
lend

Gerund
lending

Past participle
lent

like [laɪk] *mögen*

▶ Die **continuous**-Formen sind nicht gebräuchlich.

Present

	Present simple	Present continuous	Present perfect simple	Present perfect continuous
I	like		have liked	
you	like		have liked	
he/she/it	likes		has liked	
we	like		have liked	
you	like		have liked	
they	like		have liked	

Past

	Past simple	Past continuous	Past perfect simple	Past perfect continuous
I	liked		had liked	
you	liked		had liked	
he/she/it	liked		had liked	
we	liked		had liked	
you	liked		had liked	
they	liked		had liked	

Future

	Future simple	Future continuous	Future perfect simple	Future perfect continuous
I	will like		will have liked	
you	will like		will have liked	
he/she/it	will like		will have liked	
we	will like		will have liked	
you	will like		will have liked	
they	will like		will have liked	

Conditional

	Conditional	Conditional past
I	would like	would have liked
you	would like	would have liked
he/she/it	would like	would have liked
we	would like	would have liked
you	would like	would have liked
they	would like	would have liked

Imperative
like

Gerund
liking

Past participle
liked

listen ['lɪsn] *zuhören*

Present

	Present simple	Present continuous	Present perfect simple	Present perfect continuous
I	listen	am listening	have listened	have been listening
you	listen	are listening	have listened	have been listening
he/she/it	listens	is listening	has listened	has been listening
we	listen	are listening	have listened	have been listening
you	listen	are listening	have listened	have been listening
they	listen	are listening	have listened	have been listening

Past

	Past simple	Past continuous	Past perfect simple	Past perfect continuous
I	listened	was listening	had listened	had been listening
you	listened	were listening	had listened	had been listening
he/she/it	listened	was listening	had listened	had been listening
we	listened	were listening	had listened	had been listening
you	listened	were listening	had listened	had been listening
they	listened	were listening	had listened	had been listening

Future

	Future simple	Future continuous	Future perfect simple	Future perfect continuous
I	will listen	will be listening	will have listened	will have been listening
you	will listen	will be listening	will have listened	will have been listening
he/she/it	will listen	will be listening	will have listened	will have been listening
we	will listen	will be listening	will have listened	will have been listening
you	will listen	will be listening	will have listened	will have been listening
they	will listen	will be listening	will have listened	will have been listening

Conditional

	Conditional	Conditional past
I	would listen	would have listened
you	would listen	would have listened
he/she/it	would listen	would have listened
we	would listen	would have listened
you	would listen	would have listened
they	would listen	would have listened

Imperative
listen

Gerund
listening

Past participle
listened

live [lɪv] *leben*

Present

	Present simple	Present continuous	Present perfect simple	Present perfect continuous
I	live	am living	have lived	have been living
you	live	are living	have lived	have been living
he/she/it	lives	is living	has lived	has been living
we	live	are living	have lived	have been living
you	live	are living	have lived	have been living
they	live	are living	have lived	have been living

Past

	Past simple	Past continuous	Past perfect simple	Past perfect continuous
I	lived	was living	had lived	had been living
you	lived	were living	had lived	had been living
he/she/it	lived	was living	had lived	had been living
we	lived	were living	had lived	had been living
you	lived	were living	had lived	had been living
they	lived	were living	had lived	had been living

Future

	Future simple	Future continuous	Future perfect simple	Future perfect continuous
I	will live	will be living	will have lived	will have been living
you	will live	will be living	will have lived	will have been living
he/she/it	will live	will be living	will have lived	will have been living
we	will live	will be living	will have lived	will have been living
you	will live	will be living	will have lived	will have been living
they	will live	will be living	will have lived	will have been living

Conditional

	Conditional	Conditional past
I	would live	would have lived
you	would live	would have lived
he/she/it	would live	would have lived
we	would live	would have lived
you	would live	would have lived
they	would live	would have lived

Imperative
live

Gerund
living

Past participle
lived

look [lʊk] *sehen, schauen*

Present

	Present simple	Present continuous	Present perfect simple	Present perfect continuous
I	look	am looking	have looked	have been looking
you	look	are looking	have looked	have been looking
he/she/it	looks	is looking	has looked	has been looking
we	look	are looking	have looked	have been looking
you	look	are looking	have looked	have been looking
they	look	are looking	have looked	have been looking

Past

	Past simple	Past continuous	Past perfect simple	Past perfect continuous
I	looked	was looking	had looked	had been looking
you	looked	were looking	had looked	had been looking
he/she/it	looked	was looking	had looked	had been looking
we	looked	were looking	had looked	had been looking
you	looked	were looking	had looked	had been looking
they	looked	were looking	had looked	had been looking

Future

	Future simple	Future continuous	Future perfect simple	Future perfect continuous
I	will look	will be looking	will have looked	will have been looking
you	will look	will be looking	will have looked	will have been looking
he/she/it	will look	will be looking	will have looked	will have been looking
we	will look	will be looking	will have looked	will have been looking
you	will look	will be looking	will have looked	will have been looking
they	will look	will be looking	will have looked	will have been looking

Conditional

	Conditional	Conditional past
I	would look	would have looked
you	would look	would have looked
he/she/it	would look	would have looked
we	would look	would have looked
you	would look	would have looked
they	would look	would have looked

Imperative
look

Gerund
looking

Past participle
looked

make [meɪk] *machen*

Present

	Present simple	Present continuous	Present perfect simple	Present perfect continuous
I	make	am making	have made	have been making
you	make	are making	have made	have been making
he/she/it	makes	is making	has made	has been making
we	make	are making	have made	have been making
you	make	are making	have made	have been making
they	make	are making	have made	have been making

Past

	Past simple	Past continuous	Past perfect simple	Past perfect continuous
I	made	was making	had made	had been making
you	made	were making	had made	had been making
he/she/it	made	was making	had made	had been making
we	made	were making	had made	had been making
you	made	were making	had made	had been making
they	made	were making	had made	had been making

Future

	Future simple	Future continuous	Future perfect simple	Future perfect continuous
I	will make	will be making	will have made	will have been making
you	will make	will be making	will have made	will have been making
he/she/it	will make	will be making	will have made	will have been making
we	will make	will be making	will have made	will have been making
you	will make	will be making	will have made	will have been making
they	will make	will be making	will have made	will have been making

Conditional

	Conditional	Conditional past
I	would make	would have made
you	would make	would have made
he/she/it	would make	would have made
we	would make	would have made
you	would make	would have made
they	would make	would have made

Imperative
make

Gerund
making

Past participle
made

meet [mi:t] *treffen*

Present

	Present simple	Present continuous	Present perfect simple	Present perfect continuous
I	meet	am meeting	have **met**	have been meeting
you	meet	are meeting	have **met**	have been meeting
he/she/it	meet**s**	is meeting	has **met**	has been meeting
we	meet	are meeting	have **met**	have been meeting
you	meet	are meeting	have **met**	have been meeting
they	meet	are meeting	have **met**	have been meeting

Past

	Past simple	Past continuous	Past perfect simple	Past perfect continuous
I	**met**	was meeting	had **met**	had been meeting
you	**met**	were meeting	had **met**	had been meeting
he/she/it	**met**	was meeting	had **met**	had been meeting
we	**met**	were meeting	had **met**	had been meeting
you	**met**	were meeting	had **met**	had been meeting
they	**met**	were meeting	had **met**	had been meeting

Future

	Future simple	Future continuous	Future perfect simple	Future perfect continuous
I	will meet	will be meeting	will have **met**	will have been meeting
you	will meet	will be meeting	will have **met**	will have been meeting
he/she/it	will meet	will be meeting	will have **met**	will have been meeting
we	will meet	will be meeting	will have **met**	will have been meeting
you	will meet	will be meeting	will have **met**	will have been meeting
they	will meet	will be meeting	will have **met**	will have been meeting

Conditional

	Conditional	Conditional past
I	would meet	would have **met**
you	would meet	would have **met**
he/she/it	would meet	would have **met**
we	would meet	would have **met**
you	would meet	would have **met**
they	would meet	would have **met**

Imperative
meet

Gerund
meeting

Past participle
met

must [mʌst] / have to ['hæv tʊ] *müssen, (in verneinten Sätzen) dürfen*

Present

	Present simple	Present continuous	Present perfect simple	Present perfect continuous
I	must/have to	am having to	have had to	have been having to
you	must/have to	are having to	have had to	have been having to
he/she/it	must/has to	is having to	has had to	has been having to
we	must/have to	are having to	have had to	have been having to
you	must/have to	are having to	have had to	have been having to
they	must/have to	are having to	have had to	have been having to

Past

	Past simple	Past continuous	Past perfect simple	Past perfect continuous
I	had to	was having to	had had to	had been having to
you	had to	were having to	had had to	had been having to
he/she/it	had to	was having to	had had to	had been having to
we	had to	were having to	had had to	had been having to
you	had to	were having to	had had to	had been having to
they	had to	were having to	had had to	had been having to

Future

	Future simple	Future continuous	Future perfect simple	Future perfect continuous
I	will have to	will be having to	will have had to	will have been having to
you	will have to	will be having to	will have had to	will have been having to
he/she/it	will have to	will be having to	will have had to	will have been having to
we	will have to	will be having to	will have had to	will have been having to
you	will have to	will be having to	will have had to	will have been having to
they	will have to	will be having to	will have had to	will have been having to

Conditional

	Conditional	Conditional past
I	would have to	would have had to
you	would have to	would have had to
he/she/it	would have to	would have had to
we	would have to	would have had to
you	would have to	would have had to
they	would have to	would have had to

Imperative
–

Gerund
having to

Past participle
had to

pay [peɪ] *(be)zahlen*

Present

	Present simple	Present continuous	Present perfect simple	Present perfect continuous
I	pay	am paying	have paid	have been paying
you	pay	are paying	have paid	have been paying
he/she/it	pays	is paying	has paid	has been paying
we	pay	are paying	have paid	have been paying
you	pay	are paying	have paid	have been paying
they	pay	are paying	have paid	have been paying

Past

	Past simple	Past continuous	Past perfect simple	Past perfect continuous
I	paid	was paying	had paid	had been paying
you	paid	were paying	had paid	had been paying
he/she/it	paid	was paying	had paid	had been paying
we	paid	were paying	had paid	had been paying
you	paid	were paying	had paid	had been paying
they	paid	were paying	had paid	had been paying

Future

	Future simple	Future continuous	Future perfect simple	Future perfect continuous
I	will pay	will be paying	will have paid	will have been paying
you	will pay	will be paying	will have paid	will have been paying
he/she/it	will pay	will be paying	will have paid	will have been paying
we	will pay	will be paying	will have paid	will have been paying
you	will pay	will be paying	will have paid	will have been paying
they	will pay	will be paying	will have paid	will have been paying

Conditional

	Conditional	Conditional past
I	would pay	would have paid
you	would pay	would have paid
he/she/it	would pay	would have paid
we	would pay	would have paid
you	would pay	would have paid
they	would pay	would have paid

Imperative
pay

Gerund
paying

Past participle
paid

put [pʊt] *setzen, legen, stellen*

Present

	Present simple	Present continuous	Present perfect simple	Present perfect continuous
I	put	am putting	have put	have been putting
you	put	are putting	have put	have been putting
he/she/it	puts	is putting	has put	has been putting
we	put	are putting	have put	have been putting
you	put	are putting	have put	have been putting
they	put	are putting	have put	have been putting

Past

	Past simple	Past continuous	Past perfect simple	Past perfect continuous
I	put	was putting	had put	had been putting
you	put	were putting	had put	had been putting
he/she/it	put	was putting	had put	had been putting
we	put	were putting	had put	had been putting
you	put	were putting	had put	had been putting
they	put	were putting	had put	had been putting

Future

	Future simple	Future continuous	Future perfect simple	Future perfect continuous
I	will put	will be putting	will have put	will have been putting
you	will put	will be putting	will have put	will have been putting
he/she/it	will put	will be putting	will have put	will have been putting
we	will put	will be putting	will have put	will have been putting
you	will put	will be putting	will have put	will have been putting
they	will put	will be putting	will have put	will have been putting

Conditional

	Conditional	Conditional past
I	would put	would have put
you	would put	would have put
he/she/it	would put	would have put
we	would put	would have put
you	would put	would have put
they	would put	would have put

Imperative
put

Gerund
putting

Past participle
put

read [ri:d] *lesen*

Present

	Present simple	Present continuous	Present perfect simple	Present perfect continuous
I	read	am reading	have read	have been reading
you	read	are reading	have read	have been reading
he/she/it	reads	is reading	has read	has been reading
we	read	are reading	have read	have been reading
you	read	are reading	have read	have been reading
they	read	are reading	have read	have been reading

Past

	Past simple	Past continuous	Past perfect simple	Past perfect continuous
I	read	was reading	had read	had been reading
you	read	were reading	had read	had been reading
he/she/it	read	was reading	had read	had been reading
we	read	were reading	had read	had been reading
you	read	were reading	had read	had been reading
they	read	were reading	had read	had been reading

Future

	Future simple	Future continuous	Future perfect simple	Future perfect continuous
I	will read	will be reading	will have read	will have been reading
you	will read	will be reading	will have read	will have been reading
he/she/it	will read	will be reading	will have read	will have been reading
we	will read	will be reading	will have read	will have been reading
you	will read	will be reading	will have read	will have been reading
they	will read	will be reading	will have read	will have been reading

Conditional

	Conditional	Conditional past
I	would read	would have read
you	would read	would have read
he/she/it	would read	would have read
we	would read	would have read
you	would read	would have read
they	would read	would have read

Imperative
read

Gerund
reading

Past participle
read

rise [raɪz] *(an)steigen, aufstehen*

Present

	Present simple	Present continuous	Present perfect simple	Present perfect continuous
I	rise	am rising	have risen	have been rising
you	rise	are rising	have risen	have been rising
he/she/it	rises	is rising	has risen	has been rising
we	rise	are rising	have risen	have been rising
you	rise	are rising	have risen	have been rising
they	rise	are rising	have risen	have been rising

Past

	Past simple	Past continuous	Past perfect simple	Past perfect continuous
I	rose	was rising	had risen	had been rising
you	rose	were rising	had risen	had been rising
he/she/it	rose	was rising	had risen	had been rising
we	rose	were rising	had risen	had been rising
you	rose	were rising	had risen	had been rising
they	rose	were rising	had risen	had been rising

Future

	Future simple	Future continuous	Future perfect simple	Future perfect continuous
I	will rise	will be rising	will have risen	will have been rising
you	will rise	will be rising	will have risen	will have been rising
he/she/it	will rise	will be rising	will have risen	will have been rising
we	will rise	will be rising	will have risen	will have been rising
you	will rise	will be rising	will have risen	will have been rising
they	will rise	will be rising	will have risen	will have been rising

Conditional

	Conditional	Conditional past
I	would rise	would have risen
you	would rise	would have risen
he/she/it	would rise	would have risen
we	would rise	would have risen
you	would rise	would have risen
they	would rise	would have risen

Imperative
rise

Gerund
rising

Past participle
risen

run [rʌn] *laufen, rennen*

Present

	Present simple	Present continuous	Present perfect simple	Present perfect continuous
I	run	am running	have run	have been running
you	run	are running	have run	have been running
he/she/it	runs	is running	has run	has been running
we	run	are running	have run	have been running
you	run	are running	have run	have been running
they	run	are running	have run	have been running

Past

	Past simple	Past continuous	Past perfect simple	Past perfect continuous
I	ran	was running	had run	had been running
you	ran	were running	had run	had been running
he/she/it	ran	was running	had run	had been running
we	ran	were running	had run	had been running
you	ran	were running	had run	had been running
they	ran	were running	had run	had been running

Future

	Future simple	Future continuous	Future perfect simple	Future perfect continuous
I	will run	will be running	will have run	will have been running
you	will run	will be running	will have run	will have been running
he/she/it	will run	will be running	will have run	will have been running
we	will run	will be running	will have run	will have been running
you	will run	will be running	will have run	will have been running
they	will run	will be running	will have run	will have been running

Conditional

	Conditional	Conditional past
I	would run	would have run
you	would run	would have run
he/she/it	would run	would have run
we	would run	would have run
you	would run	would have run
they	would run	would have run

Imperative
run

Gerund
running

Past participle
run

say [seɪ] *sagen*

Present

	Present simple	Present continuous	Present perfect simple	Present perfect continuous
I	say	am saying	have **said**	have been saying
you	say	are saying	have **said**	have been saying
he/she/it	says	is saying	has **said**	has been saying
we	say	are saying	have **said**	have been saying
you	say	are saying	have **said**	have been saying
they	say	are saying	have **said**	have been saying

Past

	Past simple	Past continuous	Past perfect simple	Past perfect continuous
I	**said**	was saying	had **said**	had been saying
you	**said**	were saying	had **said**	had been saying
he/she/it	**said**	was saying	had **said**	had been saying
we	**said**	were saying	had **said**	had been saying
you	**said**	were saying	had **said**	had been saying
they	**said**	were saying	had **said**	had been saying

Future

	Future simple	Future continuous	Future perfect simple	Future perfect continuous
I	will say	will be saying	will have **said**	will have been saying
you	will say	will be saying	will have **said**	will have been saying
he/she/it	will say	will be saying	will have **said**	will have been saying
we	will say	will be saying	will have **said**	will have been saying
you	will say	will be saying	will have **said**	will have been saying
they	will say	will be saying	will have **said**	will have been saying

Conditional

	Conditional	Conditional past
I	would say	would have **said**
you	would say	would have **said**
he/she/it	would say	would have **said**
we	would say	would have **said**
you	would say	would have **said**
they	would say	would have **said**

Imperative
say

Gerund
saying

Past participle
said

see [si:] *sehen*

Present

	Present simple	Present continuous	Present perfect simple	Present perfect continuous
I	see	am seeing	have seen	have been seeing
you	see	are seeing	have seen	have been seeing
he/she/it	sees	is seeing	has seen	has been seeing
we	see	are seeing	have seen	have been seeing
you	see	are seeing	have seen	have been seeing
they	see	are seeing	have seen	have been seeing

Past

	Past simple	Past continuous	Past perfect simple	Past perfect continuous
I	saw	was seeing	had seen	had been seeing
you	saw	were seeing	had seen	had been seeing
he/she/it	saw	was seeing	had seen	had been seeing
we	saw	were seeing	had seen	had been seeing
you	saw	were seeing	had seen	had been seeing
they	saw	were seeing	had seen	had been seeing

Future

	Future simple	Future continuous	Future perfect simple	Future perfect continuous
I	will see	will be seeing	will have seen	will have been seeing
you	will see	will be seeing	will have seen	will have been seeing
he/she/it	will see	will be seeing	will have seen	will have been seeing
we	will see	will be seeing	will have seen	will have been seeing
you	will see	will be seeing	will have seen	will have been seeing
they	will see	will be seeing	will have seen	will have been seeing

Conditional

	Conditional	Conditional past
I	would see	would have seen
you	would see	would have seen
he/she/it	would see	would have seen
we	would see	would have seen
you	would see	would have seen
they	would see	would have seen

Imperative
see

Gerund
seeing

Past participle
seen

sell [sel] *verkaufen*

Present

	Present simple	Present continuous	Present perfect simple	Present perfect continuous
I	sell	am selling	have sold	have been selling
you	sell	are selling	have sold	have been selling
he/she/it	sells	is selling	has sold	has been selling
we	sell	are selling	have sold	have been selling
you	sell	are selling	have sold	have been selling
they	sell	are selling	have sold	have been selling

Past

	Past simple	Past continuous	Past perfect simple	Past perfect continuous
I	sold	was selling	had sold	had been selling
you	sold	were selling	had sold	had been selling
he/she/it	sold	was selling	had sold	had been selling
we	sold	were selling	had sold	had been selling
you	sold	were selling	had sold	had been selling
they	sold	were selling	had sold	had been selling

Future

	Future simple	Future continuous	Future perfect simple	Future perfect continuous
I	will sell	will be selling	will have sold	will have been selling
you	will sell	will be selling	will have sold	will have been selling
he/she/it	will sell	will be selling	will have sold	will have been selling
we	will sell	will be selling	will have sold	will have been selling
you	will sell	will be selling	will have sold	will have been selling
they	will sell	will be selling	will have sold	will have been selling

Conditional

	Conditional	Conditional past
I	would sell	would have sold
you	would sell	would have sold
he/she/it	would sell	would have sold
we	would sell	would have sold
you	would sell	would have sold
they	would sell	would have sold

Imperative
sell

Gerund
selling

Past participle
sold

send [send] *senden, schicken*

Present

	Present simple	Present continuous	Present perfect simple	Present perfect continuous
I	send	am sending	have sent	have been sending
you	send	are sending	have sent	have been sending
he/she/it	sends	is sending	has sent	has been sending
we	send	are sending	have sent	have been sending
you	send	are sending	have sent	have been sending
they	send	are sending	have sent	have been sending

Past

	Past simple	Past continuous	Past perfect simple	Past perfect continuous
I	sent	was sending	had sent	had been sending
you	sent	were sending	had sent	had been sending
he/she/it	sent	was sending	had sent	had been sending
we	sent	were sending	had sent	had been sending
you	sent	were sending	had sent	had been sending
they	sent	were sending	had sent	had been sending

Future

	Future simple	Future continuous	Future perfect simple	Future perfect continuous
I	will send	will be sending	will have sent	will have been sending
you	will send	will be sending	will have sent	will have been sending
he/she/it	will send	will be sending	will have sent	will have been sending
we	will send	will be sending	will have sent	will have been sending
you	will send	will be sending	will have sent	will have been sending
they	will send	will be sending	will have sent	will have been sending

Conditional

	Conditional	Conditional past
I	would send	would have sent
you	would send	would have sent
he/she/it	would send	would have sent
we	would send	would have sent
you	would send	would have sent
they	would send	would have sent

Imperative
send

Gerund
sending

Past participle
sent

shut [ʃʌt] *schließen, zumachen*

Present

	Present simple	Present continuous	Present perfect simple	Present perfect continuous
I	shut	am shutting	have shut	have been shutting
you	shut	are shutting	have shut	have been shutting
he/she/it	shuts	is shutting	has shut	has been shutting
we	shut	are shutting	have shut	have been shutting
you	shut	are shutting	have shut	have been shutting
they	shut	are shutting	have shut	have been shutting

Past

	Past simple	Past continuous	Past perfect simple	Past perfect continuous
I	shut	was shutting	had shut	had been shutting
you	shut	were shutting	had shut	had been shutting
he/she/it	shut	was shutting	had shut	had been shutting
we	shut	were shutting	had shut	had been shutting
you	shut	were shutting	had shut	had been shutting
they	shut	were shutting	had shut	had been shutting

Future

	Future simple	Future continuous	Future perfect simple	Future perfect continuous
I	will shut	will be shutting	will have shut	will have been shutting
you	will shut	will be shutting	will have shut	will have been shutting
he/she/it	will shut	will be shutting	will have shut	will have been shutting
we	will shut	will be shutting	will have shut	will have been shutting
you	will shut	will be shutting	will have shut	will have been shutting
they	will shut	will be shutting	will have shut	will have been shutting

Conditional

	Conditional	Conditional past
I	would shut	would have shut
you	would shut	would have shut
he/she/it	would shut	would have shut
we	would shut	would have shut
you	would shut	would have shut
they	would shut	would have shut

Imperative
shut

Gerund
shutting

Past participle
shut

sit [sɪt] *sitzen*

Present

	Present simple	Present continuous	Present perfect simple	Present perfect continuous
I	sit	am sitting	have sat	have been sitting
you	sit	are sitting	have sat	have been sitting
he/she/it	sits	is sitting	has sat	has been sitting
we	sit	are sitting	have sat	have been sitting
you	sit	are sitting	have sat	have been sitting
they	sit	are sitting	have sat	have been sitting

Past

	Past simple	Past continuous	Past perfect simple	Past perfect continuous
I	sat	was sitting	had sat	had been sitting
you	sat	were sitting	had sat	had been sitting
he/she/it	sat	was sitting	had sat	had been sitting
we	sat	were sitting	had sat	had been sitting
you	sat	were sitting	had sat	had been sitting
they	sat	were sitting	had sat	had been sitting

Future

	Future simple	Future continuous	Future perfect simple	Future perfect continuous
I	will sit	will be sitting	will have sat	will have been sitting
you	will sit	will be sitting	will have sat	will have been sitting
he/she/it	will sit	will be sitting	will have sat	will have been sitting
we	will sit	will be sitting	will have sat	will have been sitting
you	will sit	will be sitting	will have sat	will have been sitting
they	will sit	will be sitting	will have sat	will have been sitting

Conditional

	Conditional	Conditional past
I	would sit	would have sat
you	would sit	would have sat
he/she/it	would sit	would have sat
we	would sit	would have sat
you	would sit	would have sat
they	would sit	would have sat

Imperative
sit

Gerund
sitting

Past participle
sat

sleep [sli:p] *schlafen*

Present

	Present simple	Present continuous	Present perfect simple	Present perfect continuous
I	sleep	am sleeping	have slept	have been sleeping
you	sleep	are sleeping	have slept	have been sleeping
he/she/it	sleeps	is sleeping	has slept	has been sleeping
we	sleep	are sleeping	have slept	have been sleeping
you	sleep	are sleeping	have slept	have been sleeping
they	sleep	are sleeping	have slept	have been sleeping

Past

	Past simple	Past continuous	Past perfect simple	Past perfect continuous
I	slept	was sleeping	had slept	had been sleeping
you	slept	were sleeping	had slept	had been sleeping
he/she/it	slept	was sleeping	had slept	had been sleeping
we	slept	were sleeping	had slept	had been sleeping
you	slept	were sleeping	had slept	had been sleeping
they	slept	were sleeping	had slept	had been sleeping

Future

	Future simple	Future continuous	Future perfect simple	Future perfect continuous
I	will sleep	will be sleeping	will have slept	will have been sleeping
you	will sleep	will be sleeping	will have slept	will have been sleeping
he/she/it	will sleep	will be sleeping	will have slept	will have been sleeping
we	will sleep	will be sleeping	will have slept	will have been sleeping
you	will sleep	will be sleeping	will have slept	will have been sleeping
they	will sleep	will be sleeping	will have slept	will have been sleeping

Conditional

	Conditional	Conditional past
I	would sleep	would have slept
you	would sleep	would have slept
he/she/it	would sleep	would have slept
we	would sleep	would have slept
you	would sleep	would have slept
they	would sleep	would have slept

Imperative
sleep

Gerund
sleeping

Past participle
slept

speak [spi:k] *sprechen*

Present

	Present simple	Present continuous	Present perfect simple	Present perfect continuous
I	speak	am speaking	have **spoken**	have been speaking
you	speak	are speaking	have **spoken**	have been speaking
he/she/it	speak**s**	is speaking	has **spoken**	has been speaking
we	speak	are speaking	have **spoken**	have been speaking
you	speak	are speaking	have **spoken**	have been speaking
they	speak	are speaking	have **spoken**	have been speaking

Past

	Past simple	Past continuous	Past perfect simple	Past perfect continuous
I	**spoke**	was speaking	had **spoken**	had been speaking
you	**spoke**	were speaking	had **spoken**	had been speaking
he/she/it	**spoke**	was speaking	had **spoken**	had been speaking
we	**spoke**	were speaking	had **spoken**	had been speaking
you	**spoke**	were speaking	had **spoken**	had been speaking
they	**spoke**	were speaking	had **spoken**	had been speaking

Future

	Future simple	Future continuous	Future perfect simple	Future perfect continuous
I	will speak	will be speaking	will have **spoken**	will have been speaking
you	will speak	will be speaking	will have **spoken**	will have been speaking
he/she/it	will speak	will be speaking	will have **spoken**	will have been speaking
we	will speak	will be speaking	will have **spoken**	will have been speaking
you	will speak	will be speaking	will have **spoken**	will have been speaking
they	will speak	will be speaking	will have **spoken**	will have been speaking

Conditional

	Conditional	Conditional past
I	would speak	would have **spoken**
you	would speak	would have **spoken**
he/she/it	would speak	would have **spoken**
we	would speak	would have **spoken**
you	would speak	would have **spoken**
they	would speak	would have **spoken**

Imperative
speak

Gerund
speaking

Past participle
spoken

spend [spend] *ausgeben, verbringen*

Present

	Present simple	Present continuous	Present perfect simple	Present perfect continuous
I	spend	am spending	have **spent**	have been spending
you	spend	are spending	have **spent**	have been spending
he/she/it	spends	is spending	has **spent**	has been spending
we	spend	are spending	have **spent**	have been spending
you	spend	are spending	have **spent**	have been spending
they	spend	are spending	have **spent**	have been spending

Past

	Past simple	Past continuous	Past perfect simple	Past perfect continuous
I	**spent**	was spending	had **spent**	had been spending
you	**spent**	were spending	had **spent**	had been spending
he/she/it	**spent**	was spending	had **spent**	had been spending
we	**spent**	were spending	had **spent**	had been spending
you	**spent**	were spending	had **spent**	had been spending
they	**spent**	were spending	had **spent**	had been spending

Future

	Future simple	Future continuous	Future perfect simple	Future perfect continuous
I	will spend	will be spending	will have **spent**	will have been spending
you	will spend	will be spending	will have **spent**	will have been spending
he/she/it	will spend	will be spending	will have **spent**	will have been spending
we	will spend	will be spending	will have **spent**	will have been spending
you	will spend	will be spending	will have **spent**	will have been spending
they	will spend	will be spending	will have **spent**	will have been spending

Conditional

	Conditional	Conditional past
I	would spend	would have **spent**
you	would spend	would have **spent**
he/she/it	would spend	would have **spent**
we	would spend	would have **spent**
you	would spend	would have **spent**
they	would spend	would have **spent**

Imperative
spend

Gerund
spending

Past participle
spent

stand [stænd] *stehen*

Present

	Present simple	Present continuous	Present perfect simple	Present perfect continuous
I	stand	am standing	have stood	have been standing
you	stand	are standing	have stood	have been standing
he/she/it	stands	is standing	has stood	has been standing
we	stand	are standing	have stood	have been standing
you	stand	are standing	have stood	have been standing
they	stand	are standing	have stood	have been standing

Past

	Past simple	Past continuous	Past perfect simple	Past perfect continuous
I	stood	was standing	had stood	had been standing
you	stood	were standing	had stood	had been standing
he/she/it	stood	was standing	had stood	had been standing
we	stood	were standing	had stood	had been standing
you	stood	were standing	had stood	had been standing
they	stood	were standing	had stood	had been standing

Future

	Future simple	Future continuous	Future perfect simple	Future perfect continuous
I	will stand	will be standing	will have stood	will have been standing
you	will stand	will be standing	will have stood	will have been standing
he/she/it	will stand	will be standing	will have stood	will have been standing
we	will stand	will be standing	will have stood	will have been standing
you	will stand	will be standing	will have stood	will have been standing
they	will stand	will be standing	will have stood	will have been standing

Conditional

	Conditional	Conditional past
I	would stand	would have stood
you	would stand	would have stood
he/she/it	would stand	would have stood
we	would stand	would have stood
you	would stand	would have stood
they	would stand	would have stood

Imperative
stand

Gerund
standing

Past participle
stood

stay [steɪ] *bleiben*

Present

	Present simple	Present continuous	Present perfect simple	Present perfect continuous
I	stay	am staying	have stayed	have been staying
you	stay	are staying	have stayed	have been staying
he/she/it	stays	is staying	has stayed	has been staying
we	stay	are staying	have stayed	have been staying
you	stay	are staying	have stayed	have been staying
they	stay	are staying	have stayed	have been staying

Past

	Past simple	Past continuous	Past perfect simple	Past perfect continuous
I	stayed	was staying	had stayed	had been staying
you	stayed	were staying	had stayed	had been staying
he/she/it	stayed	was staying	had stayed	had been staying
we	stayed	were staying	had stayed	had been staying
you	stayed	were staying	had stayed	had been staying
they	stayed	were staying	had stayed	had been staying

Future

	Future simple	Future continuous	Future perfect simple	Future perfect continuous
I	will stay	will be staying	will have stayed	will have been staying
you	will stay	will be staying	will have stayed	will have been staying
he/she/it	will stay	will be staying	will have stayed	will have been staying
we	will stay	will be staying	will have stayed	will have been staying
you	will stay	will be staying	will have stayed	will have been staying
they	will stay	will be staying	will have stayed	will have been staying

Conditional

	Conditional	Conditional past
I	would stay	would have stayed
you	would stay	would have stayed
he/she/it	would stay	would have stayed
we	would stay	would have stayed
you	would stay	would have stayed
they	would stay	would have stayed

Imperative
stay

Gerund
staying

Past participle
stayed

stop [stɒp] *anhalten, stoppen*

Present

	Present simple	Present continuous	Present perfect simple	Present perfect continuous
I	stop	am stopping	have stopped	have been stopping
you	stop	are stopping	have stopped	have been stopping
he/she/it	stops	is stopping	has stopped	has been stopping
we	stop	are stopping	have stopped	have been stopping
you	stop	are stopping	have stopped	have been stopping
they	stop	are stopping	have stopped	have been stopping

Past

	Past simple	Past continuous	Past perfect simple	Past perfect continuous
I	stopped	was stopping	had stopped	had been stopping
you	stopped	were stopping	had stopped	had been stopping
he/she/it	stopped	was stopping	had stopped	had been stopping
we	stopped	were stopping	had stopped	had been stopping
you	stopped	were stopping	had stopped	had been stopping
they	stopped	were stopping	had stopped	had been stopping

Future

	Future simple	Future continuous	Future perfect simple	Future perfect continuous
I	will stop	will be stopping	will have stopped	will have been stopping
you	will stop	will be stopping	will have stopped	will have been stopping
he/she/it	will stop	will be stopping	will have stopped	will have been stopping
we	will stop	will be stopping	will have stopped	will have been stopping
you	will stop	will be stopping	will have stopped	will have been stopping
they	will stop	will be stopping	will have stopped	will have been stopping

Conditional

	Conditional	Conditional past
I	would stop	would have stopped
you	would stop	would have stopped
he/she/it	would stop	would have stopped
we	would stop	would have stopped
you	would stop	would have stopped
they	would stop	would have stopped

Imperative
stop

Gerund
stopping

Past participle
stopped

swim [swɪm] *schwimmen*

Present

	Present simple	Present continuous	Present perfect simple	Present perfect continuous
I	swim	am swimming	have swum	have been swimming
you	swim	are swimming	have swum	have been swimming
he/she/it	swims	is swimming	has swum	has been swimming
we	swim	are swimming	have swum	have been swimming
you	swim	are swimming	have swum	have been swimming
they	swim	are swimming	have swum	have been swimming

Past

	Past simple	Past continuous	Past perfect simple	Past perfect continuous
I	swam	was swimming	had swum	had been swimming
you	swam	were swimming	had swum	had been swimming
he/she/it	swam	was swimming	had swum	had been swimming
we	swam	were swimming	had swum	had been swimming
you	swam	were swimming	had swum	had been swimming
they	swam	were swimming	had swum	had been swimming

Future

	Future simple	Future continuous	Future perfect simple	Future perfect continuous
I	will swim	will be swimming	will have swum	will have been swimming
you	will swim	will be swimming	will have swum	will have been swimming
he/she/it	will swim	will be swimming	will have swum	will have been swimming
we	will swim	will be swimming	will have swum	will have been swimming
you	will swim	will be swimming	will have swum	will have been swimming
they	will swim	will be swimming	will have swum	will have been swimming

Conditional

	Conditional	Conditional past
I	would swim	would have swum
you	would swim	would have swum
he/she/it	would swim	would have swum
we	would swim	would have swum
you	would swim	would have swum
they	would swim	would have swum

Imperative
swim

Gerund
swimming

Past participle
swum

take [teɪk] *nehmen*

Present

	Present simple	Present continuous	Present perfect simple	Present perfect continuous
I	take	am taking	have taken	have been taking
you	take	are taking	have taken	have been taking
he/she/it	takes	is taking	has taken	has been taking
we	take	are taking	have taken	have been taking
you	take	are taking	have taken	have been taking
they	take	are taking	have taken	have been taking

Past

	Past simple	Past continuous	Past perfect simple	Past perfect continuous
I	took	was taking	had taken	had been taking
you	took	were taking	had taken	had been taking
he/she/it	took	was taking	had taken	had been taking
we	took	were taking	had taken	had been taking
you	took	were taking	had taken	had been taking
they	took	were taking	had taken	had been taking

Future

	Future simple	Future continuous	Future perfect simple	Future perfect continuous
I	will take	will be taking	will have taken	will have been taking
you	will take	will be taking	will have taken	will have been taking
he/she/it	will take	will be taking	will have taken	will have been taking
we	will take	will be taking	will have taken	will have been taking
you	will take	will be taking	will have taken	will have been taking
they	will take	will be taking	will have taken	will have been taking

Conditional

	Conditional	Conditional past
I	would take	would have taken
you	would take	would have taken
he/she/it	would take	would have taken
we	would take	would have taken
you	would take	would have taken
they	would take	would have taken

Imperative
take

Gerund
taking

Past participle
taken

tell [tel] *erzählen*

Present

	Present simple	Present continuous	Present perfect simple	Present perfect continuous
I	tell	am telling	have told	have been telling
you	tell	are telling	have told	have been telling
he/she/it	tells	is telling	has told	has been telling
we	tell	are telling	have told	have been telling
you	tell	are telling	have told	have been telling
they	tell	are telling	have told	have been telling

Past

	Past simple	Past continuous	Past perfect simple	Past perfect continuous
I	told	was telling	had told	had been telling
you	told	were telling	had told	had been telling
he/she/it	told	was telling	had told	had been telling
we	told	were telling	had told	had been telling
you	told	were telling	had told	had been telling
they	told	were telling	had told	had been telling

Future

	Future simple	Future continuous	Future perfect simple	Future perfect continuous
I	will tell	will be telling	will have told	will have been telling
you	will tell	will be telling	will have told	will have been telling
he/she/it	will tell	will be telling	will have told	will have been telling
we	will tell	will be telling	will have told	will have been telling
you	will tell	will be telling	will have told	will have been telling
they	will tell	will be telling	will have told	will have been telling

Conditional

	Conditional	Conditional past
I	would tell	would have told
you	would tell	would have told
he/she/it	would tell	would have told
we	would tell	would have told
you	would tell	would have told
they	would tell	would have told

Imperative
tell

Gerund
telling

Past participle
told

think [θɪŋk] *denken*

Present

	Present simple	Present continuous	Present perfect simple	Present perfect continuous
I	think	am thinking	have **thought**	have been thinking
you	think	are thinking	have **thought**	have been thinking
he/she/it	think**s**	is thinking	has **thought**	has been thinking
we	think	are thinking	have **thought**	have been thinking
you	think	are thinking	have **thought**	have been thinking
they	think	are thinking	have **thought**	have been thinking

Past

	Past simple	Past continuous	Past perfect simple	Past perfect continuous
I	**thought**	was thinking	had **thought**	had been thinking
you	**thought**	were thinking	had **thought**	had been thinking
he/she/it	**thought**	was thinking	had **thought**	had been thinking
we	**thought**	were thinking	had **thought**	had been thinking
you	**thought**	were thinking	had **thought**	had been thinking
they	**thought**	were thinking	had **thought**	had been thinking

Future

	Future simple	Future continuous	Future perfect simple	Future perfect continuous
I	will think	will be thinking	will have **thought**	will have been thinking
you	will think	will be thinking	will have **thought**	will have been thinking
he/she/it	will think	will be thinking	will have **thought**	will have been thinking
we	will think	will be thinking	will have **thought**	will have been thinking
you	will think	will be thinking	will have **thought**	will have been thinking
they	will think	will be thinking	will have **thought**	will have been thinking

Conditional

	Conditional	Conditional past
I	would think	would have **thought**
you	would think	would have **thought**
he/she/it	would think	would have **thought**
we	would think	would have **thought**
you	would think	would have **thought**
they	would think	would have **thought**

Imperative
think

Gerund
thinking

Past participle
thought

throw [θrəʊ] *werfen*

Present

	Present simple	Present continuous	Present perfect simple	Present perfect continuous
I	throw	am throwing	have **thrown**	have been throwing
you	throw	are throwing	have **thrown**	have been throwing
he/she/it	throws	is throwing	has **thrown**	has been throwing
we	throw	are throwing	have **thrown**	have been throwing
you	throw	are throwing	have **thrown**	have been throwing
they	throw	are throwing	have **thrown**	have been throwing

Past

	Past simple	Past continuous	Past perfect simple	Past perfect continuous
I	**threw**	was throwing	had **thrown**	had been throwing
you	**threw**	were throwing	had **thrown**	had been throwing
he/she/it	**threw**	was throwing	had **thrown**	had been throwing
we	**threw**	were throwing	had **thrown**	had been throwing
you	**threw**	were throwing	had **thrown**	had been throwing
they	**threw**	were throwing	had **thrown**	had been throwing

Future

	Future simple	Future continuous	Future perfect simple	Future perfect continuous
I	will throw	will be throwing	will have **thrown**	will have been throwing
you	will throw	will be throwing	will have **thrown**	will have been throwing
he/she/it	will throw	will be throwing	will have **thrown**	will have been throwing
we	will throw	will be throwing	will have **thrown**	will have been throwing
you	will throw	will be throwing	will have **thrown**	will have been throwing
they	will throw	will be throwing	will have **thrown**	will have been throwing

Conditional

	Conditional	Conditional past
I	would throw	would have **thrown**
you	would throw	would have **thrown**
he/she/it	would throw	would have **thrown**
we	would throw	would have **thrown**
you	would throw	would have **thrown**
they	would throw	would have **thrown**

Imperative
throw

Gerund
throwing

Past participle
thrown

travel ['trævl] *reisen*

Present

	Present simple	Present continuous	Present perfect simple	Present perfect continuous
I	travel	am travelling	have travelled	have been travelling
you	travel	are travelling	have travelled	have been travelling
he/she/it	travels	is travelling	has travelled	has been travelling
we	travel	are travelling	have travelled	have been travelling
you	travel	are travelling	have travelled	have been travelling
they	travel	are travelling	have travelled	have been travelling

Past

	Past simple	Past continuous	Past perfect simple	Past perfect continuous
I	travelled	was travelling	had travelled	had been travelling
you	travelled	were travelling	had travelled	had been travelling
he/she/it	travelled	was travelling	had travelled	had been travelling
we	travelled	were travelling	had travelled	had been travelling
you	travelled	were travelling	had travelled	had been travelling
they	travelled	were travelling	had travelled	had been travelling

Future

	Future simple	Future continuous	Future perfect simple	Future perfect continuous
I	will travel	will be travelling	will have travelled	will have been travelling
you	will travel	will be travelling	will have travelled	will have been travelling
he/she/it	will travel	will be travelling	will have travelled	will have been travelling
we	will travel	will be travelling	will have travelled	will have been travelling
you	will travel	will be travelling	will have travelled	will have been travelling
they	will travel	will be travelling	will have travelled	will have been travelling

Conditional

	Conditional	Conditional past
I	would travel	would have travelled
you	would travel	would have travelled
he/she/it	would travel	would have travelled
we	would travel	would have travelled
you	would travel	would have travelled
they	would travel	would have travelled

Imperative
travel

Gerund
travelling / traveling (AE)

Past participle
travelled / traveled (AE)

visit ['vɪzɪt] *besuchen*

Present

	Present simple	Present continuous	Present perfect simple	Present perfect continuous
I	visit	am visiting	have visited	have been visiting
you	visit	are visiting	have visited	have been visiting
he/she/it	visits	is visiting	has visited	has been visiting
we	visit	are visiting	have visited	have been visiting
you	visit	are visiting	have visited	have been visiting
they	visit	are visiting	have visited	have been visiting

Past

	Past simple	Past continuous	Past perfect simple	Past perfect continuous
I	visited	was visiting	had visited	had been visiting
you	visited	were visiting	had visited	had been visiting
he/she/it	visited	was visiting	had visited	had been visiting
we	visited	were visiting	had visited	had been visiting
you	visited	were visiting	had visited	had been visiting
they	visited	were visiting	had visited	had been visiting

Future

	Future simple	Future continuous	Future perfect simple	Future perfect continuous
I	will visit	will be visiting	will have visited	will have been visiting
you	will visit	will be visiting	will have visited	will have been visiting
he/she/it	will visit	will be visiting	will have visited	will have been visiting
we	will visit	will be visiting	will have visited	will have been visiting
you	will visit	will be visiting	will have visited	will have been visiting
they	will visit	will be visiting	will have visited	will have been visiting

Conditional

	Conditional	Conditional past
I	would visit	would have visited
you	would visit	would have visited
he/she/it	would visit	would have visited
we	would visit	would have visited
you	would visit	would have visited
they	would visit	would have visited

Imperative
visit

Gerund
visiting

Past participle
visited

wear [wɛə] *tragen*

Present

	Present simple	Present continuous	Present perfect simple	Present perfect continuous
I	wear	am wearing	have worn	have been wearing
you	wear	are wearing	have worn	have been wearing
he/she/it	wears	is wearing	has worn	has been wearing
we	wear	are wearing	have worn	have been wearing
you	wear	are wearing	have worn	have been wearing
they	wear	are wearing	have worn	have been wearing

Past

	Past simple	Past continuous	Past perfect simple	Past perfect continuous
I	wore	was wearing	had worn	had been wearing
you	wore	were wearing	had worn	had been wearing
he/she/it	wore	was wearing	had worn	had been wearing
we	wore	were wearing	had worn	had been wearing
you	wore	were wearing	had worn	had been wearing
they	wore	were wearing	had worn	had been wearing

Future

	Future simple	Future continuous	Future perfect simple	Future perfect continuous
I	will wear	will be wearing	will have worn	will have been wearing
you	will wear	will be wearing	will have worn	will have been wearing
he/she/it	will wear	will be wearing	will have worn	will have been wearing
we	will wear	will be wearing	will have worn	will have been wearing
you	will wear	will be wearing	will have worn	will have been wearing
they	will wear	will be wearing	will have worn	will have been wearing

Conditional

	Conditional	Conditional past
I	would wear	would have worn
you	would wear	would have worn
he/she/it	would wear	would have worn
we	would wear	would have worn
you	would wear	would have worn
they	would wear	would have worn

Imperative
wear

Gerund
wearing

Past participle
worn

write [raɪt] *schreiben*

Present

	Present simple	Present continuous	Present perfect simple	Present perfect continuous
I	write	am writing	have **written**	have been writing
you	write	are writing	have **written**	have been writing
he/she/it	writes	is writing	has **written**	has been writing
we	write	are writing	have **written**	have been writing
you	write	are writing	have **written**	have been writing
they	write	are writing	have **written**	have been writing

Past

	Past simple	Past continuous	Past perfect simple	Past perfect continuous
I	**wrote**	was writing	had **written**	had been writing
you	**wrote**	were writing	had **written**	had been writing
he/she/it	**wrote**	was writing	had **written**	had been writing
we	**wrote**	were writing	had **written**	had been writing
you	**wrote**	were writing	had **written**	had been writing
they	**wrote**	were writing	had **written**	had been writing

Future

	Future simple	Future continuous	Future perfect simple	Future perfect continuous
I	will write	will be writing	will have **written**	will have been writing
you	will write	will be writing	will have **written**	will have been writing
he/she/it	will write	will be writing	will have **written**	will have been writing
we	will write	will be writing	will have **written**	will have been writing
you	will write	will be writing	will have **written**	will have been writing
they	will write	will be writing	will have **written**	will have been writing

Conditional

	Conditional	Conditional past
I	would write	would have **written**
you	would write	would have **written**
he/she/it	would write	would have **written**
we	would write	would have **written**
you	would write	would have **written**
they	would write	would have **written**

Imperative
write

Gerund
writing

Past participle
written

Liste der unregelmäßigen Verben

Die folgende Liste enthält die wichtigsten unregelmäßigen Verben des Englischen. Ein Verb ist im Englischen unregelmäßig, wenn sein **past simple** und/oder **past participle** nicht durch Anhängen von **-(e)d** an die Grundform gebildet wird. Einige Verben weisen neben einer unregelmäßigen Form auch eine regelmäßige auf. Diese ist durch Schrägstrich nach der unregelmäßigen Form aufgeführt. Die blau markierten unregelmäßigen Verben sind besonders geläufig und werden deshalb in den Verbtabellen in allen Formen konjugiert. In der ersten Spalte steht die **Grundform** des Verbs, in der zweiten das **past simple** und in der dritten das **past participle**. Die Lautschrift in den eckigen Klammern entspricht der Aussprache der aktuellen britischen Standardsprache (= **received pronunciation**). **AE** bedeutet **American English**.

A

arise [ə'raɪz]	arose [ə'rəʊz]	arisen [ə'rɪzn]	entstehen
awake [ə'weɪk]	awoke [ə'wəʊk]	awoken [ə'wəʊkən]	erwachen

B

be [bi:]	was [wɒz] bzw. were [wɜ:]	been [bi:n]	sein, werden
bear [beə]	bore [bɔ:]	borne [bɔ:n] / born [bɔ:n] (= geboren)	(er)tragen, gebären
beat [bi:t]	beat [bi:t]	beaten [bi:tn]	schlagen
become [bɪ'kʌm]	became [bɪ'keɪm]	become [bɪ'kʌm]	werden
begin [bɪ'gɪn]	began [bɪ'gæn]	begun [bɪ'gʌn]	beginnen
bend [bend]	bent [bent]	bent [bent]	(sich) biegen
bet [bet]	bet [bet]	bet [bet]	wetten
bid [bɪd]	bid [bɪd]	bid [bɪd]	bieten
bind [baɪnd]	bound [baʊnd]	bound [baʊnd]	binden
bite [baɪt]	bit [bɪt]	bitten ['bɪtn]	beißen
bleed [bli:d]	bled [bled]	bled [bled]	bluten
blow [bləʊ]	blew [blu:]	blown [bləʊn]	blasen
break [breɪk]	broke [brəʊk]	broken ['brəʊkn]	(zer)brechen
breed [bri:d]	bred [bred]	bred [bred]	züchten
bring [brɪŋ]	brought [brɔ:t]	brought [brɔ:t]	bringen
broadcast ['brɔ:dcɑ:st]	broadcast ['brɔ:dkɑ:st] / broadcasted ['brɔ:dkɑ:stɪd]	broadcast ['brɔ:dkɑ:st] / broadcasted ['brɔ:dkɑ:stɪd]	im Radio senden
build [bɪld]	built [bɪlt]	built [bɪlt]	bauen
burn [bɜ:n]	burnt [bɜ:nt] / burned [bɜ:nd]	burnt [bɜ:nt] / burned [bɜ:nd]	(ver)brennen
burst [bɜ:st]	burst [bɜ:st]	burst [bɜ:st]	platzen
buy [baɪ]	bought [bɔ:t]	bought [bɔ:t]	kaufen

C

cast [kɑ:st]	cast [kɑ:st]	cast [kɑ:st]	werfen
catch [kætʃ]	caught [kɔ:t]	caught [kɔ:t]	fangen
choose [tʃu:z]	chose [tʃəʊz]	chosen ['tʃəʊzn]	(aus)wählen
cling [klɪŋ]	clung [klʌŋ]	clung [klʌŋ]	sich klammern, haften
come [kʌm]	came [keɪm]	come [kʌm]	kommen
cost [kɒst]	cost [kɒst]	cost [kɒst]	kosten
creep [kri:p]	crept [krept]	crept [krept]	kriechen
cut [kʌt]	cut [kʌt]	cut [kʌt]	schneiden

D

deal [di:l]	dealt [delt]	dealt [delt]	handeln
dig [dɪg]	dug [dʌg]	dug [dʌg]	graben
do [du:]	did [dɪd]	done [dʌn]	machen, tun
draw [drɔ:]	drew [dru:]	drawn [drɔ:n]	ziehen, zeichnen
dream [dri:m]	dreamt [dremt] / dreamed [dri:md]	dreamt [dremt] / dreamed [dri:md]	träumen
drink [drɪŋk]	drank [dræŋk]	drunk [drʌŋk]	trinken
drive [draɪv]	drove [drəʊv]	driven ['drɪvn]	fahren
dwell [dwel]	dwelt [dwelt] / dwelled [dweld]	dwelt [dwelt] / dwelled [dweld]	wohnen

E

eat [i:t]	ate [et] / [eɪt]	eaten ['i:tn]	essen

F

fall [fɔ:l]	fell [fel]	fallen ['fɔ:lən]	fallen
feed [fi:d]	fed [fed]	fed [fed]	füttern
feel [fi:l]	felt [felt]	felt [felt]	fühlen
fight [faɪt]	fought [fɔ:t]	fought [fɔ:t]	kämpfen
find [faɪnd]	found [faʊnd]	found [faʊnd]	finden
flee [fli:]	fled [fled]	fled [fled]	fliehen
fling [flɪŋ]	flung [flʌŋ]	flung [flʌŋ]	werfen, schleudern
fly [flaɪ]	flew [flu:]	flown [fləʊn]	fliegen
forbid [fə'bɪd]	forbade [fə'bæd] / [fə'beɪd]	forbidden [fə'bɪdn]	verbieten
forecast ['fɔ:kɑ:st]	forecast ['fɔ:kɑ:st] / forecasted ['fɔ:kɑ:stɪd]	forecast ['fɔ:kɑ:st] / forecasted ['fɔ:kɑ:stɪd]	vorhersagen
foresee [fɔ:'si:]	foresaw [fɔ:'sɔ:]	foreseen [fɔ:'si:n]	vorhersehen
foretell [fɔ:'tel]	foretold [fɔ:'təʊld]	foretold [fɔ:'təʊld]	vorhersagen
forget [fə'get]	forgot [fə'gɒt]	forgotten [fə'gɒtn]	vergessen
forgive [fə'gɪv]	forgave [fə'geɪv]	forgiven [fə'gɪvn]	verzeihen
freeze [fri:z]	froze [frəʊz]	frozen ['frəʊzn]	(ge)frieren

G			
get [get]	got [gɒt]	got [gɒt] / (AE) gotten ['gɒtn]	bekommen
give [gɪv]	gave [geɪv]	given ['gɪvn]	geben
go [gəʊ]	went [went]	gone [gɒn]	gehen, fahren
grind [graɪnd]	ground [graʊnd]	ground [graʊnd]	(zer)mahlen
grow [grəʊ]	grew [gru:]	grown [grəʊn]	wachsen
H			
hang [hæŋ]	hung [hʌŋ] / hanged [hæŋd] (= erhängte)	hung [hʌŋ] / hanged [hæŋd] (= erhängt)	(auf)hängen, erhängen
have [hæv]	had [hæd]	had [hæd]	haben
hear [hɪə]	heard [hɜ:d]	heard [hɜ:d]	hören
hide [haɪd]	hid [hɪd]	hidden ['hɪdn]	(sich) verstecken
hit [hɪt]	hit [hɪt]	hit [hɪt]	treffen, schlagen
hold [həʊld]	held [held]	held [held]	halten
hurt [hɜ:t]	hurt [hɜ:t]	hurt [hɜ:t]	verletzen
K			
keep [ki:p]	kept [kept]	kept [kept]	behalten
kneel [ni:l]	knelt [nelt] / (AE auch) kneeled [ni:ld]	knelt [nelt] / (AE auch) kneeled [ni:ld]	knien
know [nəʊ]	knew [nju:]	known [nəʊn]	wissen, kennen
L			
lay [leɪ]	laid [leɪd]	laid [leɪd]	legen
lead [li:d]	led [led]	led [led]	führen
lean [li:n]	leant [lent] / leaned [li:nd]	leant [lent] / leaned [li:nd]	lehnen
leap [li:p]	leapt [lept] / leaped [li:pd]	leapt [lept] / leaped [li:pd]	springen
learn [lɜ:n]	learnt [lɜ:nt] / learned [lɜ:nd]	learnt [lɜ:nt] / learned [lɜ:nd]	lernen
leave [li:v]	left [left]	left [left]	(ver)lassen
lend [lend]	lent [lent]	lent [lent]	(aus)leihen
let [let]	let [let]	let [let]	lassen
lie [laɪ]	lay [leɪ]	lain [leɪn]	liegen
light [laɪt]	lit [lɪt] / lighted ['laɪtɪd]	lit [lɪt] / lighted ['laɪtɪd]	anzünden
lose [lu:z]	lost [lɒst]	lost [lɒst]	verlieren

M

make [meɪk]	made [meɪd]	made [meɪd]	machen
mean [mi:n]	meant [ment]	meant [ment]	bedeuten, meinen
meet [mi:t]	met [met]	met [met]	treffen, begegnen
mistake [mɪ'steɪk]	mistook [mɪ'stʊk]	mistaken [mɪ'steɪkən]	missverstehen
mow [məʊ]	mowed [məʊd]	mown [məʊn] / mowed [məʊd]	mähen

P

pay [peɪ]	paid [peɪd]	paid [peɪd]	(be)zahlen
put [pʊt]	put [pʊt]	put [pʊt]	setzen, stellen, legen

Q

quit [kwɪt]	quit [kwɪt] / quitted ['kwɪtɪd]	quit [kwɪt] / quitted ['kwɪtɪd]	verlassen, aufhören

R

read [ri:d]	read [red]	read [red]	lesen
ride [raɪd]	rode [rəʊd]	ridden ['rɪdn]	reiten, fahren
ring [rɪŋ]	rang [ræŋ]	rung [rʌŋ]	läuten, anrufen
rise [raɪz]	rose [rəʊz]	risen ['rɪzn]	(an)steigen, aufstehen
run [rʌn]	ran [ræn]	run [rʌn]	rennen

S

saw [sɔ:]	sawed [sɔ:d]	sawn [sɔ:n] / (AE auch) sawed [sɔ:d]	sägen
say [seɪ]	said [sed]	said [sed]	sagen
see [si:]	saw [sɔ:]	seen [si:n]	sehen
seek [si:k]	sought [sɔ:t]	sought [sɔ:t]	suchen
sell [sel]	sold [səʊld]	sold [səʊld]	verkaufen
send [send]	sent [sent]	sent [sent]	senden, schicken
set [set]	set [set]	set [set]	setzen, stellen
sew [səʊ]	sewed [səʊd]	sewn [səʊn] / (AE auch) sewed [soʊd]	nähen
shake [ʃeɪk]	shook [ʃʊk]	shaken ['ʃeɪkn]	schütteln
shed [ʃed]	shed [ʃed]	shed [ʃed]	(Blut) vergießen, (Blätter) abwerfen
shine [ʃaɪn]	shone [ʃɒn] / shined [ʃaɪnd] (= putzte Schuhe)	shone [ʃɒn] / shined [ʃaɪnd] (= Schuhe geputzt)	scheinen, glänzen, Schuhe putzen
shoot [ʃu:t]	shot [ʃɒt]	shot [ʃɒt]	(er)schießen
show [ʃəʊ]	showed [ʃəʊd]	shown [ʃəʊn]	zeigen
shrink [ʃrɪŋk]	shrank [ʃræŋk] / shrunk [ʃrʌŋk]	shrunk [ʃrʌŋk]	eingehen, schrumpfen
shut [ʃʌt]	shut [ʃʌt]	shut [ʃʌt]	schließen, zumachen

sing [sɪŋ]	sang [sæŋ]	sung [sʌŋ]	singen
sink [sɪŋk]	sank [sæŋk]	sunk [sʌŋk]	sinken
sit [sɪt]	sat [sæt]	sat [sæt]	sitzen
sleep [sli:p]	slept [slept]	slept [slept]	schlafen
slide [slaɪd]	slid [slɪd]	slid [slɪd]	gleiten
slit [slɪt]	slit [slɪt]	slit [slɪt]	(auf)schlitzen
smell [smel]	smelt [smelt] / smelled [smeld]	smelt [smelt] / smelled [smeld]	riechen
sow [səʊ]	sowed [səʊd]	sown [səʊn] / (AE auch) sewed [soʊd]	säen
speed [spi:d]	sped [sped] / speeded [spi:dɪd] (= fuhr zu schnell)	sped [sped] / speeded ['spi:dɪd] (= zu schnell gefahren)	rasen, zu schnell fahren
speak [spi:k]	spoke [spəʊk]	spoken ['spəʊkən]	sprechen
spell [spel]	spelt [spelt] / spelled [speld]	spelt [spelt] / spelled [speld]	buchstabieren
spend [spend]	spent [spent]	spent [spent]	ausgeben, verbringen
spill [spɪl]	spilt [spɪlt] / spilled [spɪld]	spilt [spɪlt] / spilled [spɪld]	verschütten
spin [spɪn]	spun [spʌn]	spun [spʌn]	spinnen, (sich) schnell drehen
spit [spɪt]	spat [spæt] / (AE auch) spit [spɪt]	spat [spæt] / (AE auch) spit [spɪt]	spucken
spoil [spɔɪl]	spoilt [spɔɪlt] / spoiled [spɔɪld]	spoilt [spɔɪlt] / spoiled [spɔɪld]	verderben
spread [spred]	spread [spred]	spread [spred]	verbreiten
spring [sprɪŋ]	sprang [spræŋ] / (AE auch) sprung [sprʌŋ]	sprung [sprʌŋ]	springen
stand [stænd]	stood [stʊd]	stood [stʊd]	stehen
steal [sti:l]	stole [stəʊl]	stolen [stəʊlən]	stehlen
stick [stɪk]	stuck [stʌk]	stuck [stʌk]	kleben, stecken
sting [stɪŋ]	stung [stʌŋ]	stung [stʌŋ]	stechen
stink [stɪŋk]	stank [stæŋk]	stunk [stʌŋk]	stinken
stride [straɪd]	strode [strəʊd]	strode [strəʊd]	schreiten
strike [straɪk]	struck [strʌk]	struck [strʌk] / (AE auch) stricken ['strɪkən]	schlagen, treffen
strive [straɪv]	strove [strəʊv]	striven ['strɪvən]	streben
swear [sweə]	swore [swɔ:]	sworn [swɔ:n]	schwören
sweep [swi:p]	swept [swept]	swept [swept]	kehren
swim [swɪm]	swam [swæm]	swum [swʌm]	schwimmen
swing [swɪŋ]	swung [swʌŋ]	swung [swʌŋ]	schwingen

T

take [teɪk]	took [tʊk]	taken [teɪkn]	nehmen
teach [ti:tʃ]	taught [tɔ:t]	taught [tɔ:t]	lehren
tear [teə]	tore [tɔ:]	torn [tɔ:n]	zerreißen
tell [tel]	told [təʊld]	told [təʊld]	erzählen
think [θɪŋk]	thought [θɔ:t]	thought [θɔ:t]	denken
throw [θrəʊ]	threw [θru:]	thrown [θrəʊn]	werfen
tread [tred]	trod [trɒd]	trodden ['trɒdn]	treten

U

understand [ˌʌndə'stænd]	understood [ˌʌndə'stʊd]	understood [ˌʌndə'stʊd]	verstehen
upset [ˌʌp'set]	upset [ˌʌp'set]	upset [ˌʌp'set]	umstoßen, aufregen

W

wake [weɪk]	woke [wəʊk]	woken ['wəʊkn]	aufwachen, wecken
wear [weə]	wore [wɔ:]	worn [wɔ:n]	tragen
weave [wi:v]	wove [wəʊv]	woven ['wəʊvn]	weben
wed [wed]	wed [wed] / wedded ['wedɪd]	wed [wed] / wedded ['wedɪd]	heiraten
weep [wi:p]	wept [wept]	wept [wept]	weinen
win [wɪn]	won [wʌn]	won [wʌn]	gewinnen
wind [waɪnd]	wound [waʊnd]	wound [waʊnd]	wickeln
withdraw [wɪð'drɔ:]	withdrew [wɪð'dru:]	withdrawn [wɪð'drɔ:n]	(sich) zurückziehen
wring [rɪŋ]	wrung [rʌŋ]	wrung [rʌŋ]	auswringen
write [raɪt]	wrote [rəʊt]	written ['rɪtn]	schreiben

Alphabetisches Verbregister Deutsch – Englisch

Der Pfeil verweist auf die Seite, auf der das Verb konjugiert wird. **AE** bedeutet **American English**.

A

B

D

E

F

G

T

V

W

Z

Notizen

Notizen

Notizen

Notizen

Notizen

Notizen

Notizen

Notizen

Notizen

Notizen

Notizen

Notizen

Notizen

Notizen

Notizen

Notizen

Notizen

Notizen

Notizen

Notizen

Notizen

Notizen

Notizen

Notizen

Notizen